Assessment Book

PEARSON
Scott
Foresman

Editorial Offices: Glenview, Illinois • Parsippany, New Jersey • New York, New York
Sales Offices: Parsippany, New Jersey • Duluth, Georgia • Glenview, Illinois •
Coppell, Texas • Ontario, California • Mesa, Arizona

www.sfsocialstudies.com

Program Authors

Dr. Candy Dawson Boyd
Professor, School of Education
Director of Reading Programs
St. Mary's College
Moraga, California

Dr. Geneva Gay
Professor of Education
University of Washington
Seattle, Washington

Rita Geiger
Director of Social Studies and
   Foreign Languages
Norman Public Schools
Norman, Oklahoma

Dr. James B. Kracht
Associate Dean for
   Undergraduate Programs
   and Teacher Education
College of Education
Texas A&M University
College Station, Texas

Dr. Valerie Ooka Pang
Professor of Teacher Education
San Diego State University
San Diego, California

Dr. C. Frederick Risinger
Director, Professional
   Development and Social
   Studies Education
Indiana University
Bloomington, Indiana

Sara Miranda Sanchez
Elementary and Early
   Childhood Curriculum
   Coordinator
Albuquerque Public Schools
Albuquerque, New Mexico

Contributing Authors

Dr. Carol Berkin
Professor of History
Baruch College and the
   Graduate Center
The City University of New York
New York, New York

Lee A. Chase
Staff Development Specialist
Chesterfield County
   Public Schools
Chesterfield County, Virginia

Dr. Jim Cummins
Professor of Curriculum
Ontario Institute for Studies
   in Education
University of Toronto
Toronto, Canada

Dr. Allen D. Glenn
Professor and Dean Emeritus
Curriculum and Instruction
College of Education
University of Washington
Seattle, Washington

Dr. Carole L. Hahn
Professor, Educational Studies
Emory University
Atlanta, Georgia

Dr. M. Gail Hickey
Professor of Education
Indiana University-Purdue
   University
Fort Wayne, Indiana

Dr. Bonnie Meszaros
Associate Director
Center for Economic Education
   and Entrepreneurship
University of Delaware
Newark, Delaware

ISBN 0-328-08194-9

2 3 4 5 6 7 8 9 10-V016-12 11 10 09 08 07 06 05 04

© Scott Foresman 3

Contents

To the Teacher

One way to evaluate the success of your social studies instruction lies in using the assessment options provided in **Scott Foresman** *Social Studies.* These options will help you measure students' progress toward social studies instructional goals.

The assessment tools provided with **Scott Foresman** *Social Studies* can

- help you determine which students need more help and where classroom instruction needs to be reinforced, reviewed, or expanded.
- help you evaluate how well students comprehend, communicate, and apply what they have learned.

Scott Foresman *Social Studies* provides a comprehensive assessment package as shown below.

Assessment Options Available in Scott Foresman *Social Studies*

Formal Assessments	Lesson Reviews, PE/TE Chapter Reviews, PE/TE Chapter Tests, Assessment Book Unit Review, PE/TE Unit Tests, Assessment Book Test Talk Practice Book ExamView® Test Bank CD-ROM
Informal Assessments	Teacher's Edition Questions Section Reviews, PE/TE Close and Assess, TE Ongoing Assessments, TE
Portfolio Assessments	Portfolio Assessments, TE Leveled Practice, TE Workbook Pages Chapter Review: Write About History, PE/TE Unit Review: Apply Skills, PE/TE Curriculum Connection: Writing, PE/TE
Performance Assessments	Hands-on Unit Project, PE/TE Internet Activity, PE Chapter Performance Assessment, TE Unit Review: Write and Share, PE/TE Scoring Guides, TE

© Scott Foresman 3

Overview of the Assessment Book

Chapter and Unit Tests

The Chapter and Unit Tests are tools to evaluate students' understanding of critical social studies concepts and their ability to apply and analyze them. There is a four-page, reproducible test for each chapter and unit in the Student Book.

Students are asked to fill in blanks, complete sentences, choose a correct answer from a series of possible responses, draw an answer, match items, and read/complete a map, chart, or graph. There is an answer key for each Chapter and Unit Test at the back of the Assessment Book.

Chapter and Unit Content Tests

The two-page content test includes a series of multiple choice questions covering levels of thinking from knowledge to comprehension, application, and analysis. Each question is correlated to a student learning objective.

Chapter and Unit Skills Tests

The two-page skills test checks students' knowledge of and ability to apply the social studies skills taught in the Student Book. Each question is correlated to a specific thinking skill.

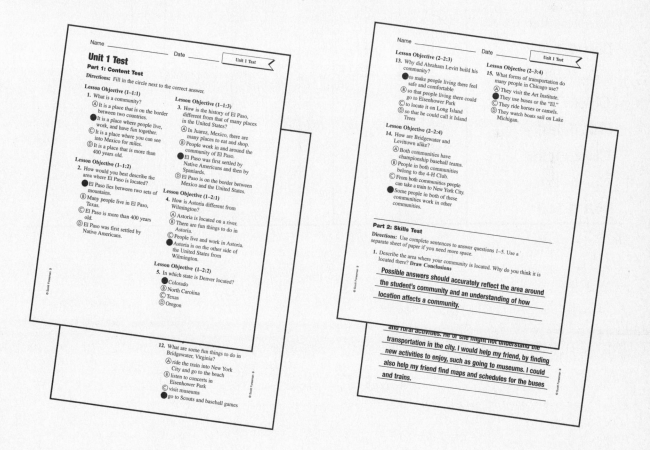

Class Record Sheet

Student Names										
Chapter 1 Test										
Chapter 2 Test										
Unit 1 Test										
Chapter 3 Test										
Chapter 4 Test										
Unit 2 Test										
Chapter 5 Test										
Chapter 6 Test										
Unit 3 Test										
Chapter 7 Test										
Chapter 8 Test										
Unit 4 Test										
Chapter 9 Test										
Chapter 10 Test										
Unit 5 Test										
Chapter 11 Test										
Chapter 12 Test										
Unit 6 Test										

Class Record Sheet

Student Names

Chapter 1 Test									
Chapter 2 Test									
Unit 1 Test									
Chapter 3 Test									
Chapter 4 Test									
Unit 2 Test									
Chapter 5 Test									
Chapter 6 Test									
Unit 3 Test									
Chapter 7 Test									
Chapter 8 Test									
Unit 4 Test									
Chapter 9 Test									
Chapter 10 Test									
Unit 5 Test									
Chapter 11 Test									
Chapter 12 Test									
Unit 6 Test									

NOTES

Chapter 1 Test

Part 1: Content Test

Directions: Fill in the circle next to the correct answer.

1. What is a community?
   - (A) where people live, work, and have fun together
   - (B) where people visit on vacation
   - (C) where people go to work
   - (D) where people cross a bridge over the Rio Grande

2. Which sentence tells something about the history of El Paso, Texas?
   - (A) It was first settled by Native Americans and then by the Spanish.
   - (B) People work and have fun together in El Paso.
   - (C) El Paso is Spanish and means "the pass."
   - (D) Carlos lives in the community of El Paso, Texas.

3. Where is the community of El Paso, Texas, located?
   - (A) near beautiful lakes
   - (B) between two sets of mountains
   - (C) where two rivers meet
   - (D) in a desert region

4. Which detail supports the following main idea? **There are many fun things to do and see in El Paso.**
   - (A) From Rim Road you can see into Mexico for miles.
   - (B) Carlos's parents vote for people who want to help the community.
   - (C) Letter carriers deliver the mail in El Paso.
   - (D) El Paso is more than 400 years old.

5. In which state is Astoria located?
   - (A) Colorado
   - (B) Texas
   - (C) North Carolina
   - (D) Oregon

6. Which main idea does the following detail support? **Farming communities are located in areas with rich soil.**
   - (A) Anna lives in Astoria.
   - (B) Astoria is almost 200 years old.
   - (C) Anna's cousins live in Denver.
   - (D) Communities are located in special places.

© Scott Foresman 3

7. Which detail supports the following main idea? **The Pacific Ocean is important to the community of Astoria.**

   Ⓐ Astoria has many historical museums to visit.

   Ⓑ Astoria is on the other side of the United States from Wilmington.

   Ⓒ People in Astoria like to fish, swim, boat, and ride the waves.

   Ⓓ Astoria holds a special celebration in June.

8. How would you best describe the area where Wilmington is located?

   Ⓐ It is between the Cape Fear River and the Atlantic Ocean.

   Ⓑ It was first settled by Native Americans.

   Ⓒ It is where Anna's grandparents live.

   Ⓓ It is a dot on a map.

9. Who settled in Wilmington after the Native Americans?

   Ⓐ English
   Ⓑ Arapaho
   Ⓒ Texans
   Ⓓ Norwegians

10. How are Denver, Colorado, and Wilmington, North Carolina, alike?

    Ⓐ They are both located in the Rocky Mountains.

    Ⓑ They both were settled by Native Americans.

    Ⓒ They both are near Bald Head Island.

    Ⓓ Gold brought prospectors to both communities.

11. What are some things that culture includes?

    Ⓐ computers and textbooks
    Ⓑ parks, stores, and hospitals
    Ⓒ language, food, and holidays
    Ⓓ mountains, rivers, and oceans

12. Which of these describes a part of the culture of Timbuktu, Mali?

    Ⓐ Mali is located in West Africa.

    Ⓑ Merchants once did lots of business in Timbuktu.

    Ⓒ The main language in Mali is French.

    Ⓓ The sun shines brightly almost every day in Mali.

13. How is Timbuktu today like it was in the past?

Ⓐ Religion is still very important to the people of Timbuktu.

Ⓑ Today many thousands of people live in Timbuktu.

Ⓒ Timbuktu is still a center of learning.

Ⓓ Camels carry blocks of salt to and from the city.

14. What might you have seen in Timbuktu four to six centuries ago?

Ⓐ camels carrying goods on their backs

Ⓑ the only two mosques in the city

Ⓒ fewer people than you see today

Ⓓ rain falling every day

Part 2: Skills Test

Directions: Use complete sentences to answer questions 1–4. Use a separate sheet of paper if you need more space.

1. Give three details to support the following main idea: **Many people work together to make El Paso a special community. Main Idea and Details**

_____

_____

_____

_____

2. Describe the area where your community is located. How might its location help it grow in the future? **Predict**

_____

_____

_____

3. How did Denver first begin? How did it grow? Write the events of Denver's history in order. **Sequence**

_____

_____

_____

4. Suppose that you are to take a trip to Timbuktu, Mali. What is the weather like there? What should you plan to take with you? **Solve Problems**

_____

_____

_____

The United States

5. Use the map to answer the questions. **Use Map Scales**
   a. What is a map scale?

_____

_____

   b. How many miles does 1 inch represent on the map scale?

_____

   c. About how many kilometers wide is the state of Wyoming?

_____

Chapter 2 Test

Part 1: Content Test

Directions: Fill in the circle next to the correct answer.

1. How would you describe a rural community?
   - Ⓐ The towns are small and far apart.
   - Ⓑ The towns are very big.
   - Ⓒ The towns have many people living in them.
   - Ⓓ There are no towns in a rural community.

2. What are rural communities usually surrounded by?
   - Ⓐ many houses
   - Ⓑ open lands and fields
   - Ⓒ deserts and mountains
   - Ⓓ water

3. How would you describe the area where Bridgewater is located?
   - Ⓐ It is located between two sets of mountains.
   - Ⓑ It is located in the Rocky Mountains.
   - Ⓒ It is located in a desert in West Africa.
   - Ⓓ It is located on the North River in the Shenandoah Valley.

4. What are some fun things to do in Bridgewater, Virginia?
   - Ⓐ go to the beach
   - Ⓑ go to Scouts and 4-H Club
   - Ⓒ visit museums
   - Ⓓ ski down mountains

5. Which detail supports the following main idea? **If you like sports, Bridgewater is the place for you.**
   - Ⓐ The 4-H Club meets once a month to talk about farm issues.
   - Ⓑ Amy has lots of friends.
   - Ⓒ Bridgewater became the name of the town in 1835.
   - Ⓓ The Bridgewater All-Star baseball team has won the Virginia state championship.

6. How is a suburban community different from a rural community?
   - Ⓐ Suburban communities have homes.
   - Ⓑ Suburban communities have stores.
   - Ⓒ Suburban communities are located near large cities.
   - Ⓓ Suburban communities have fun things to do.

© Scott Foresman 3

7. Which main idea is supported by the following detail? **Levittown is just a train ride from New York City**.

Ⓐ Abraham Levitt began building homes in 1947.

Ⓑ Levittown, New York, is a suburb of New York City.

Ⓒ William Levitt helped his father plan and build their community.

Ⓓ New York City is the largest city in the United States.

8. How are Levittown and Wilmington alike?

Ⓐ They both are located near the Atlantic Ocean.

Ⓑ They both are rural communities.

Ⓒ They both are located in North Carolina.

Ⓓ They both were started by Abraham Levitt.

9. Why do people form communities?

Ⓐ They want to live and work where they feel safe and comfortable.

Ⓑ They like to grow potatoes.

Ⓒ They want to ride the train to the city.

Ⓓ They like to listen to concerts.

10. How did Abraham Levitt and his family change a rural potato farm into a suburb?

Ⓐ They built many houses, schools, and parks.

Ⓑ They called their community Island Trees.

Ⓒ They rode the train to New York City.

Ⓓ They visited Jones Beach State Park.

11. How is an urban community similar to a rural community?

Ⓐ Both have plenty of things to do.

Ⓑ Both have similar amounts of people.

Ⓒ Both have similar types of buildings.

Ⓓ Both have similar amounts of open land.

12. Which detail supports the following main idea? **People in Chicago work in many places.**

Ⓐ The "El" is the elevated train that runs through Chicago.

Ⓑ In 1837 the town got the name *Chicago*.

Ⓒ Chicago has large department stores, banks, and office buildings.

Ⓓ Chicago is in the midwest part of the United States.

© Scott Foresman 3

13. How is Chicago different from Levittown?

Ⓐ There are homes, parks, and places of worship in Chicago.

Ⓑ People in Chicago drive cars to work.

Ⓒ Chicago is a great place to live.

Ⓓ Chicago is an important center of population and business activity.

15. What fun thing can you do in Chicago that you cannot do in Bridgewater?

Ⓐ attend 4-H meetings

Ⓑ visit the Art Institute

Ⓒ help others in your community

Ⓓ go to Scouts

14. How are Chicago and Bridgewater alike?

Ⓐ There are fun things to do in both communities.

Ⓑ They are both suburban communities.

Ⓒ They are both large cities.

Ⓓ They both are located in the same state.

Part 2: Skills Test

Directions: Use complete sentences to answer questions 1–5. Use a separate sheet of paper if you need more space.

1. Give three details to support the following main idea: **Bridgewater is a great place to live and go to school. Main Idea and Details**

_____

_____

_____

_____

_____

2. Write one fact and one opinion about Bridgewater, Virginia. Do you think that Amy likes living in her community? **Why? Fact and Opinion**

_____

_____

_____

_____

3. Suppose your family is moving to a community where children enjoy going to 4-H Club meetings. What type of community might you be moving to? What will the towns be like there? What else might you and your friends do for fun? **Make Inferences**

_____

_____

_____

_____

4. Why is Lake Michigan important to Beth and her family? How do you know? **Draw Conclusions**

_____

_____

_____

5. Suppose that one day the train system in Chicago stopped working. What might this mean for the people of that city? **Cause and Effect**

_____

_____

_____

_____

© Scott Foresman 3

Unit 1 Test

Part 1: Content Test

Directions: Fill in the circle next to the correct answer.

1. What is a community?

   Ⓐ It is a place that is on the border between two countries.

   Ⓑ It is a place where people live, work, and have fun together.

   Ⓒ It is a place where you can see into Mexico for miles.

   Ⓓ It is a place that is more than 400 years old.

2. How would you best describe the area where El Paso is located?

   Ⓐ El Paso lies between two sets of mountains.

   Ⓑ Many people live in El Paso

   Ⓒ El Paso is more than 400 years old.

   Ⓓ El Paso was first settled by Native Americans.

3. How is the history of El Paso different from that of many places in the United States?

   Ⓐ In Juarez, Mexico, there are many places to eat and shop.

   Ⓑ People work in and around the community of El Paso.

   Ⓒ El Paso was first settled by Native Americans and then by Spaniards.

   Ⓓ El Paso is on the border between Mexico and the United States.

4. How is Astoria different from Wilmington?

   Ⓐ Astoria is located on a river.

   Ⓑ There are fun things to do in Astoria.

   Ⓒ People live and work in Astoria.

   Ⓓ Astoria is on the other side of the United States from Wilmington.

5. In which state is Denver located?

   Ⓐ Colorado

   Ⓑ North Carolina

   Ⓒ Texas

   Ⓓ Oregon

6. Which detail supports the following main idea? **Wilmington has some really cool places to visit.**

   Ⓐ Visitors can go to Fort Fisher, a sand fort.

   Ⓑ Wilmington is located in the state of North Carolina.

   Ⓒ Anna's grandparents live in Wilmington.

   Ⓓ A dot on the map shows where Wilmington is located.

© Scott Foresman 3

7. Where did the first settlers of Astoria move there from?

Ⓐ Spain

Ⓑ Arapaho

Ⓒ Texas

Ⓓ Scandinavia

8. Which of the following is NOT a part of culture?

Ⓐ food

Ⓑ clothing

Ⓒ language

Ⓓ weather

9. How has Timbuktu changed from earlier times?

Ⓐ Today Timbuktu is located on the continent of Africa.

Ⓑ Today many fewer people live in Timbuktu.

Ⓒ Today Timbuktu is located in a desert.

Ⓓ Today there are beautiful mosques in Timbuktu.

10. What was Timbuktu like from the year 1400 to about 1600?

Ⓐ It was a very wealthy city.

Ⓑ It had only two great mosques.

Ⓒ Very few people lived there.

Ⓓ It was located in the United States of America.

11. Where are rural communities located?

Ⓐ near large cities

Ⓑ by the water

Ⓒ in a desert

Ⓓ in the countryside

12. What are some fun things to do in Bridgewater, Virginia?

Ⓐ ride the train into New York City and go to the beach

Ⓑ listen to concerts in Eisenhower Park

Ⓒ visit museums

Ⓓ go to Scouts and baseball games

13. How are Bridgewater and Levittown alike?

Ⓐ Both communities have championship baseball teams.

Ⓑ People in both communities belong to the 4-H Club.

Ⓒ From both communities people can take a train to New York City.

Ⓓ Some people in both of these communities work in other communities.

14. Why did Abraham Levitt build his community?

   Ⓐ to make people living there feel safe and comfortable

   Ⓑ so that people living there could go to Eisenhower Park

   Ⓒ to locate it on Long Island

   Ⓓ so that he could call it Island Trees

15. What forms of transportation do many people in Chicago use?

   Ⓐ They visit the Art Institute.

   Ⓑ They use buses or the "El."

   Ⓒ They ride horses or camels.

   Ⓓ They watch boats sail on Lake Michigan.

Part 2: Skills Test

Directions: Use complete sentences to answer questions 1–3. Use a separate sheet of paper if you need more space.

1. Describe the area where your community is located. Why do you think it is located there? **Draw Conclusions**

_____

_____

_____

_____

2. How did Denver's location help it grow? **Cause and Effect**

_____

_____

_____

_____

3. How has Timbuktu changed between the year 1400 and today? **Compare and Contrast**

_____

_____

_____

The Local Community

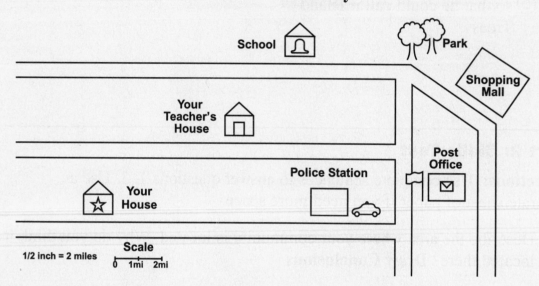

4. Use the map to answer the questions. **Use Map Scales**
   a. How is a map scale useful?

_____

   b. How many miles does 1 inch represent on the map scale?

_____

   c. How many miles is the trip from your house to the school?

_____

Chapter 3 Test

Part 1: Content Test

Directions: Fill in the circle next to the correct answer.

1. How is Tom similar to some students in his new class in Boston?
   - Ⓐ Tom was born in Boston.
   - Ⓑ Tom has always lived in Boston.
   - Ⓒ Tom moved to Boston from someplace else.
   - Ⓓ Tom does not live in Boston.

2. How is Tom different from some students in his new class in Boston?
   - Ⓐ Tom has not always lived in Boston.
   - Ⓑ Tom has always lived in Boston.
   - Ⓒ Tom has always lived outside the United States.
   - Ⓓ Tom does not live in Boston.

3. How is Tom's family similar to some families that move to the United States from other countries?
   - Ⓐ Tom's family moved for freedom of religion.
   - Ⓑ Tom's family moved for freedom of speech.
   - Ⓒ Tom's family had to learn a new language.
   - Ⓓ Tom's family moved because of a job.

4. What can Nicole's new friends in Boston help her learn?
   - Ⓐ soccer
   - Ⓑ English
   - Ⓒ Haitian Creole
   - Ⓓ Haitian customs

5. What is similar between Haiti and the United States?
   - Ⓐ school
   - Ⓑ language
   - Ⓒ customs
   - Ⓓ neighborhoods

6. What have Nicole and members of her ethnic group brought from Haiti to the United States?
   - Ⓐ They brought their schools and buses.
   - Ⓑ They left all of their customs behind in Haiti.
   - Ⓒ They brought English and American foods.
   - Ⓓ They brought their language and other customs.

7. Which of the following is NOT a reason why immigrants formed communities in the United States?

   (A) to feel safe

   (B) to escape new opportunities

   (C) to set up good laws

   (D) to make their lives better

8. How can you tell that people in the United States come from different cultures and countries?

   (A) They speak many languages.

   (B) They go to the same schools.

   (C) They play soccer together.

   (D) They eat similar foods.

9. What are relatives that lived in past times called?

   (A) immigrants

   (B) ancestors

   (C) friends

   (D) parents

10. From which country did few people immigrate to the United States between 1861 and 1890?

   (A) Germany

   (B) Ireland

   (C) Mexico

   (D) Sweden

11. Why is it important for citizens of the United States to vote?

   (A) They can help make decisions that affect the community.

   (B) They can live in apartments in ethnic neighborhoods.

   (C) They can play games and sports brought to the United States by other groups.

   (D) They can move from one part of the country to another in search of an opportunity.

12. How is education today different from education in the past?

   (A) Today children learn science.

   (B) Today children learn mathematics.

   (C) Today children begin school at a young age.

   (D) Today children learn about computers.

13. What took place during the Great Migration?

   (A) Many African Americans moved to the South.

   (B) Many African Americans moved to the North.

   (C) Many African Americans moved to farms.

   (D) Many African Americans moved to other countries.

Part 2: Skills Test

Directions: Use complete sentences to answer questions 1–5. Use a separate sheet of paper if you need more space.

1. Suppose that you and your family have lived in another country and are now moving to the United States. How do you think life will change? How might it remain the same? **Make Inferences**

   _____

   _____

   _____

   _____

2. How are your community and Nicole's ethnic neighborhood different? How are they alike? **Compare and Contrast**

   _____

   _____

   _____

   _____

3. What are some positive reasons to live in an ethnic neighborhood? Do you think there are any negative reasons? If so, what are they? **Express Ideas**

   _____

   _____

   _____

   _____

4. Why do you think the Statue of Liberty is a symbol of freedom for many people? **Interpret National Symbols**

_____

_____

_____

_____

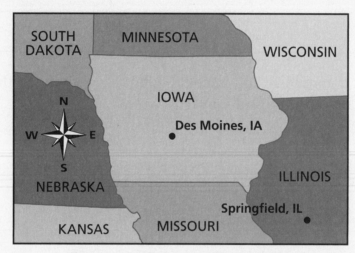

Iowa and Surrounding States

5. Use the map to answer the questions. **Use Intermediate Directions**
   a. What is an intermediate direction?

_____

   b. What state is northwest of Iowa?

_____

   c. If you drove from Des Moines, Iowa to Springfield, Illinois, in what direction would you be traveling?

_____

Chapter 4 Test

Part 1: Content Test

Directions: Fill in the circle next to the correct answer.

1. Which holiday celebrates the end of Ramadan?
   - Ⓐ Eid-al-Fitr
   - Ⓑ Christmas
   - Ⓒ Hanukkah
   - Ⓓ Kwanzaa

2. Why do many families celebrate Kwanzaa?
   - Ⓐ They like to light candles and sing songs.
   - Ⓑ They enjoy giving gifts to family members.
   - Ⓒ They want to honor their ancestors.
   - Ⓓ They are hungry for a large meal with special sweets.

3. How is Christmas different from Kwanzaa?
   - Ⓐ Families light red, green, and black candles for Christmas.
   - Ⓑ Christmas honors African American culture.
   - Ⓒ Christmas lasts for seven days.
   - Ⓓ Families decorate trees and celebrate the birth of Jesus on Christmas.

4. How are Christmas, Hanukkah, and Eid-al-Fitr alike?
   - Ⓐ Families light eight candles during all three holidays.
   - Ⓑ Families celebrate for seven days during all three holidays.
   - Ⓒ Families share a special meal or eat special foods at all three holidays.
   - Ⓓ Families decorate trees for all three holidays.

5. What do people celebrate on St. Patrick's Day?
   - Ⓐ a corn harvest
   - Ⓑ green clothing
   - Ⓒ life in Europe
   - Ⓓ Irish culture

6. How are Cinco de Mayo and St. Patrick's Day alike?
   - Ⓐ People eat green-dyed food to celebrate both.
   - Ⓑ They both show that people are proud of their culture.
   - Ⓒ They are both celebrated on the fifth of May.
   - Ⓓ They both started in the country of Ireland.

© Scott Foresman 3

7. What makes the heritage festival in New Orleans unique?

    Ⓐ It honors the history and culture of the people of New Orleans.

    Ⓑ It honors the person who started New Orleans.

    Ⓒ It honors the work people in Louisiana have done that year.

    Ⓓ It celebrates the harvest.

8. Why do many communities hold their own special celebrations?

    Ⓐ to show livestock to the community members

    Ⓑ to pass out ribbons to winners of contests

    Ⓒ to celebrate the corn harvest

    Ⓓ to bring the people of the community together

9. What special event is held each year in Hutchinson, Kansas?

    Ⓐ state fair

    Ⓑ heritage festival

    Ⓒ jazz festival

    Ⓓ world's fair

10. On what day do we honor people who fought and died for the United States?

    Ⓐ the fifth of May

    Ⓑ the third Monday in January

    Ⓒ the third Thursday in November

    Ⓓ the last Monday in May

11. What two holidays honor people who fought for the United States?

    Ⓐ Memorial Day and Thanksgiving Day

    Ⓑ Veterans Day and Memorial Day

    Ⓒ Cinco de Mayo and Veterans Day

    Ⓓ Memorial Day and St. Patrick's Day

12. What did Dr. King fight for?

    Ⓐ He fought for a holiday held the third Monday in January.

    Ⓑ He fought for all people to be treated equally.

    Ⓒ He fought for freedom for the United States.

    Ⓓ He fought for the freedom to choose the government.

13. What was the name of the drive that Dr. Martin Luther King, Jr., led?

Ⓐ African Americans

Ⓑ Thanksgiving

Ⓒ Civil Rights Movement

Ⓓ Memorial Day

14. What did Dr. King use to convince people to make changes?

Ⓐ computers

Ⓑ fists

Ⓒ bombs

Ⓓ words

Part 2: Skills Test

Directions: Use complete sentences to answer questions 1–4. Use a separate sheet of paper if you need more space.

1. Why do you think many families celebrate holidays by sharing a special meal? **Draw Conclusions**

_____

_____

_____

_____

_____

2. Cinco de Mayo, Memorial Day, and Veterans Day all honor people who have fought in battles. Why do you think communities find it important to remember them? **Make Inferences**

_____

_____

_____

_____

3. The United States has a national holiday to honor Dr. Martin Luther King, Jr. Think of another person, either living or dead, whom you believe should have his or her own holiday. Why should that person have a day in his or her honor? **Express Ideas**

_____

_____

_____

4. What is your favorite holiday? Compare and contrast it with one of the holidays from your textbook. **Compare and Contrast**

_____

_____

_____

Western Hemisphere

Eastern Hemisphere

5. Use the globes to find the continents in the table. Then fill in the table to show in which hemispheres each continent is located. **Understand Hemispheres**

Continent	Northern or Southern Hemisphere	Eastern or Western Hemisphere
North America		
Asia		
South America		
Europe		

Unit 2 Test

Part 1: Content Test

Directions: Fill in the circle next to the correct answer.

1. What do many people who move to a new city have in common with many who move to a new country?

   Ⓐ Both want to find a better life.

   Ⓑ Both want to become U.S. citizens.

   Ⓒ Both want to find religious freedom.

   Ⓓ Both want to stay in their neighborhood.

2. Why do people set up systems of laws in their communities?

   Ⓐ to make the community safe

   Ⓑ to make new friends in their community

   Ⓒ to go to a new school in the community

   Ⓓ to find a better job in the community

3. Which of the following does NOT show that the United States is home to many cultures?

   Ⓐ different languages

   Ⓑ different clothing

   Ⓒ different foods

   Ⓓ different communities

4. How do ethnic neighborhoods help people who move to this country?

   Ⓐ People can learn English very quickly since that is the only language spoken in an ethnic neighborhood.

   Ⓑ People can buy American foods in an ethnic neighborhood in the United States.

   Ⓒ People can get used to a new culture while still being around their old culture.

   Ⓓ People can ride buses and talk to friends from their home country on the phone.

5. What is the word for "relatives who lived in past times"?

   Ⓐ decades

   Ⓑ symbols

   Ⓒ ancestors

   Ⓓ immigrants

6. For what reason have Tom's family and many other families moved to a new city?

   Ⓐ for a better job

   Ⓑ to get a health test

   Ⓒ to see Ellis Island

   Ⓓ to become famous writers

7. What is a benefit of becoming a citizen of the United States?

Ⓐ A citizen can vote to help make decisions.

Ⓑ A citizen can visit the museum at Ellis Island.

Ⓒ A citizen can learn a new language.

Ⓓ A citizen can migrate from one part of the country to another.

8. What made Langston Hughes famous?

Ⓐ dancing

Ⓑ writing

Ⓒ singing

Ⓓ painting

9. What is celebrated on St. Patrick's Day?

Ⓐ Jewish ancestors

Ⓑ Christian families

Ⓒ Irish culture

Ⓓ jazz music

10. What is special about Hutchinson, Kansas?

Ⓐ Pilgrims settled there.

Ⓑ The New Orleans Jazz and Heritage Festival is held there.

Ⓒ The Kansas State Fair is held there.

Ⓓ The Tomb of the Unknown Soldier is located there.

11. How is the Kansas State Fair like the New Orleans Jazz and Heritage Festival?

Ⓐ They both honor the history of the people of New Orleans.

Ⓑ They both bring the people of the community together.

Ⓒ They both celebrate the hard work of the people of Kansas.

Ⓓ They both are held in September, when the crops are ready to eat.

12. Who do Americans honor on Memorial Day and Veterans Day?

Ⓐ the people who fought for the United States

Ⓑ the leaders of the Civil Rights Movement

Ⓒ the Wampanoag Indians

Ⓓ the settlers of Plymouth

13. Why do Americans celebrate the life of Dr. Martin Luther King, Jr.?

Ⓐ He painted a famous picture of George Washington.

Ⓑ He fought for freedom for the United States.

Ⓒ He fought for all people to be treated equally.

Ⓓ He helped the Pilgrims grow their crops.

© Scott Foresman 3

Part 2: Skills Test

Directions: Use complete sentences to answer questions 1–3. Use a separate sheet of paper if you need more space.

1. Tom and Nicole both just moved to Boston. Which one might find the move more difficult? Why? How might they help each other with their new life in Boston? **Hypothesize**

_____

_____

_____

2. How were the immigrants of the early 1900s similar to and different from the African Americans of the Great Migration? **Compare and Contrast**

_____

_____

_____

_____

3. Why do communities hold special celebrations? What effect do these festivals and fairs have on life in the community? **Cause and Effect**

_____

_____

_____

_____

NEW YORK

Lake Erie

OHIO

N
NW   NE
W   E
SW   SE
S

PENNSYLVANIA

NEW
JERSEY

WEST
VIRGINIA

DELAWARE

MARYLAND

4. Use the map to answer the questions. **Use Intermediate Directions**
   a. What does the compass rose on the bottom left corner tell you? What are
   the four intermediate directions?

_____

_____

b. What state is southwest of Pennsylvania? _____

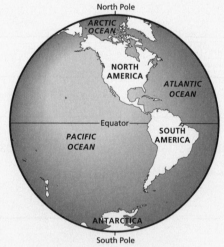

Western Hemisphere

Eastern Hemisphere

5. Study the globes and then answer the questions. **Understand Hemispheres**
   a. What two hemispheres does the equator separate?

_____

b. Which continents are in both the Northern and Southern Hemispheres?

_____

Chapter 5 Test

Part 1: Content Test

Directions: Fill in the circle next to the correct answer.

1. Which community is in the Western region of the United States?
   - (A) Stamford, Connecticut
   - (B) Charleston, South Carolina
   - (C) Bozeman, Montana
   - (D) Omaha, Nebraska

2. Which of these is a landform that you can see in the Southwest region of the United States?
   - (A) cactuses
   - (B) snakes
   - (C) canyons
   - (D) bridges

3. Farmers in the Southwest region bring in water for their crops. How has this changed their region?
   - (A) Many plants that could not grow there now grow very well.
   - (B) Many plants have died from too much water.
   - (C) Many trees have been cut to clear land for planting crops.
   - (D) Many plants cannot live there because of the cold weather.

4. How is the physical environment in Omaha, Nebraska, different from that in Bozeman, Montana?
   - (A) Omaha has no mountains.
   - (B) A river runs through Omaha.
   - (C) The weather in Omaha is cold all year long.
   - (D) Omaha has many mountains.

5. What have people done to forests to meet human needs?
   - (A) They bring in water so the trees can grow.
   - (B) They heat their homes and offices.
   - (C) They wear warm clothing, such as hats and scarves.
   - (D) They cut the trees to use for lumber to build houses.

6. Why is the climate in Kauai, Hawaii, different from the climate in Barrow, Alaska?
   - (A) Kauai is much higher than Barrow.
   - (B) Kauai is much farther away from the equator than Barrow.
   - (C) Barrow is in the Northeast region.
   - (D) Kauai is much closer to the equator than Barrow.

© Scott Foresman 3

7. Which should you NOT take to wear on a vacation in Kauai?

Ⓐ a bathing suit

Ⓑ a winter coat

Ⓒ sunglasses

Ⓓ shorts and T-shirts

8. Which activity might people living in Barrow NOT enjoy doing there?

Ⓐ ice skating

Ⓑ snow skiing

Ⓒ swimming outdoors

Ⓓ snow mobiling

9. How have the Pueblo adapted to the climate in Taos?

Ⓐ They wear warm coats all year long.

Ⓑ They make beautiful pottery to sell in the markets.

Ⓒ They live on the plateau surrounded by mountains.

Ⓓ They have built adobe houses with thick walls.

10. Which was an important natural resource in California?

Ⓐ oil

Ⓑ miners

Ⓒ homes

Ⓓ gold

11. How were the settlers at Angel's Camp different from the people of Beaumont, Texas?

Ⓐ At Angel's Camp, they dug deep into the earth looking for gold.

Ⓑ At Angel's Camp, they drilled wells looking for pockets of oil.

Ⓒ The settlers moved to Angel's Camp to work in the oil fields.

Ⓓ The settlers called what they had found "black gold."

12. What are two ways to conserve natural resources?

Ⓐ use as much of them as you can and recycle them

Ⓑ dig deep into the earth and use less of them

Ⓒ recycle them and dig oil wells

Ⓓ use less of them and recycle them

13. What would happen if we used up all the fuels on Earth?

Ⓐ We would have to find new sources of energy.

Ⓑ We would stay warm in our heated homes.

Ⓒ We would have all the light we needed.

Ⓓ We would have to look for more gold and salt.

Part 2: Skills Test

Directions: Use complete sentences to answer questions 1–4. Use a separate sheet of paper if you need more space.

1. Suppose that you live in a region with many forests, hills, and mountains. What problems might you face in trying to build roads and railways there? How can you solve those problems? **Solve Problems**

   _____

   _____

   _____

   _____

   _____

2. What is the physical environment of your community like? Describe its landforms and climate, as well as the plants, animals, and resources that can be found there. **Apply Information**

   _____

   _____

   _____

3. Which region of the United States would you most like to live in? Why? **Express Ideas**

   _____

   _____

   _____

   _____

4. What type of people moved to California in search of gold? Describe someone who would follow the Gold Rush. **Draw Conclusions**

_____

_____

_____

_____

5. Use the graph to answer the questions. **Use a Line Graph**
   a. What does the graph show?

_____

_____

   b. What do the numbers on the side of the graph tell you?

_____

   c. Which month has the warmest high temperature? What is that temperature?

_____

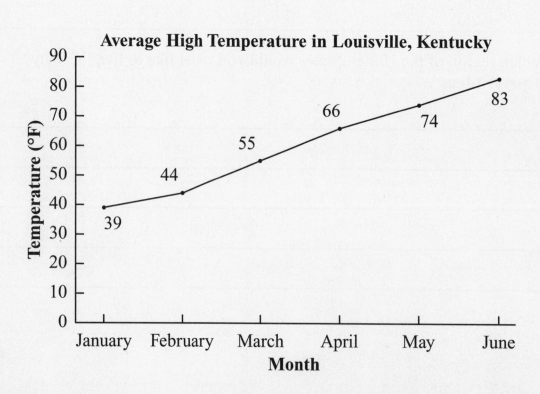

Average High Temperature in Louisville, Kentucky

© Scott Foresman 3

Chapter 6 Test

Part 1: Content Test

Directions: Fill in the circle next to the correct answer.

1. Who set up Fort Defiance and then later named it Glenwood Springs?
   - Ⓐ Glenwood Canyon
   - Ⓑ the Ute Indians
   - Ⓒ Captain Isaac Cooper
   - Ⓓ Colorado Midland Railroad

2. How did the railroad help the community of Glenwood Springs?
   - Ⓐ Miners had a way to send their coal to other communities.
   - Ⓑ Miners were able to dig for materials from the earth.
   - Ⓒ The land was able to be settled by the Ute Indians.
   - Ⓓ The community changed its name to Fort Defiance.

3. Why was it hard for railroad workers to build tracks into Glenwood Springs?
   - Ⓐ They had to build around the hot water springs.
   - Ⓑ They had to build through the desert.
   - Ⓒ They had to cut down trees to build through the forest.
   - Ⓓ They had to build through the mountains.

4. Which type of person would be most able to start a mountain community?
   - Ⓐ an impatient person
   - Ⓑ a patient person
   - Ⓒ a tired person
   - Ⓓ a lazy person

5. What happened in 1851 to make the city of Seattle start to grow?
   - Ⓐ One of the Native American leaders was Chief Sealth.
   - Ⓑ Puget Sound is located near the Pacific Ocean.
   - Ⓒ The area around Seattle has many trees.
   - Ⓓ A group of settlers built a town on Alki Point.

6. Which of these is NOT an important natural resource in Seattle?
   - Ⓐ water
   - Ⓑ gold
   - Ⓒ trees
   - Ⓓ fish

© Scott Foresman 3

7. Why did the settlers name their town in honor of Chief Sealth?

Ⓐ He was friendly to them and helped them.

Ⓑ He built all of their houses for them.

Ⓒ He showed them how to cook fish.

Ⓓ He moved to Puget Sound to be near them.

8. What became an important industry around Seattle because of a natural resource there?

Ⓐ fishing

Ⓑ computer building

Ⓒ logging

Ⓓ airplane making

9. How did the water around Seattle help it grow?

Ⓐ Its port is a place where ships come and go from around the world.

Ⓑ Airplane making and computer companies need water to build their products.

Ⓒ People who enjoy water sports moved to Seattle to be near the ocean.

Ⓓ Loggers can make money and build their businesses by sailing on the ocean.

10. What might happen to the water around Seattle if the city continues to grow?

Ⓐ The people who live in Seattle might someday use all the natural resources, including the water.

Ⓑ Computer companies will become larger.

Ⓒ The ships that come to the port and the people who live in Seattle might pollute the water.

Ⓓ The loggers might use up all of the water by cutting down trees and making lumber.

11. What happened to Indianapolis in 1820 that is still true today?

Ⓐ It became a crossroads center.

Ⓑ The Miami Indians farmed there.

Ⓒ The National Road was built.

Ⓓ It became the state capital.

12. How did the National Road help the people of the United States?

Ⓐ People from the North moved south using the road.

Ⓑ People from the East moved west using the road.

Ⓒ People from the West moved east using the road.

Ⓓ People could travel around Indianapolis more easily.

© Scott Foresman 3

13. What is one way that you CANNOT reach the city of Indianapolis?

Ⓐ by boat
Ⓑ by train
Ⓒ by car
Ⓓ by truck

14. Why did Indianapolis become a crossroads center?

Ⓐ It had the first U.S. highway and now has seven highways leading out of the city.
Ⓑ It is located in the middle of the state.
Ⓒ It is an area where the Miami and Delaware Indians farmed.
Ⓓ It is in Indiana, and it was a stop on the Underground Railroad.

15. What station of the Underground Railroad was located in Indianapolis?

Ⓐ the Bethel AME Church
Ⓑ the National Road
Ⓒ the Union Rail Station
Ⓓ the White River

Part 2: Skills Test

Directions: Use complete sentences to answer questions 1–5. Use a separate sheet of paper if you need more space.

1. How did building Fort Defiance affect the lives of the miners in Glenwood Canyon? **Make Inferences**

_____

_____

_____

_____

_____

© Scott Foresman 3

2. Describe key events in the history of Indianapolis. Write about them in the order they happened. **Sequence**

_____

_____

_____

_____

_____

3. Why do you think a station on the Underground Railroad was located in Indianapolis? **Draw Conclusions**

_____

_____

_____

4. What is special about the physical environment of your community? Is it in the mountains or near water? How and why do you think your community's founders chose the location of your community? **Apply Information**

_____

_____

_____

5. In which type of community would you rather live: a mountain community, a community near water, or a crossroads community? Why? **Express Ideas**

_____

_____

_____

Unit 3 Test

Part 1: Content Test

Directions: Fill in the circle next to the correct answer.

1. Which of these is a community in the Midwest region of the United States?
   Ⓐ Omaha, Nebraska
   Ⓑ Bozeman, Montana
   Ⓒ Kauai, Hawaii
   Ⓓ Tucson, Arizona

2. How are the landforms in Bozeman different from those in Omaha?
   Ⓐ The land around Bozeman is flat.
   Ⓑ Bozeman is surrounded by a desert.
   Ⓒ A river runs through the town of Bozeman.
   Ⓓ Bozeman is surrounded by mountains.

3. What fun activity are people NOT able to enjoy in Omaha, Nebraska?
   Ⓐ walking along paths
   Ⓑ boating on the ocean
   Ⓒ biking in the town
   Ⓓ playing in the park

4. Which landform makes it possible for people in the Western region to enjoy snow skiing?
   Ⓐ plateau
   Ⓑ desert
   Ⓒ mountain
   Ⓓ canyon

5. What important change to the environment do the farmers of the Southwest region make?
   Ⓐ They cut down trees to build their houses.
   Ⓑ They build railroads through the canyons.
   Ⓒ They bring in water to help grow their crops.
   Ⓓ They dig for minerals to feed their crops.

6. What is one way to conserve natural resources?
   Ⓐ by using as much of them as you can
   Ⓑ by using less of them
   Ⓒ by using more of them
   Ⓓ by using them only once

© Scott Foresman 3

7. Why is it important to conserve fuels?

   (A) Conserving fuels helps scientists find new sources of energy.

   (B) Once fuel is recycled, it can never be used again.

   (C) There are so many fuels that it is not possible to use them up.

   (D) Fuels are natural resources that can become used up.

8. What did Captain Isaac Cooper do to help the area of Glenwood Canyon?

   (A) He set up Fort Defiance.

   (B) He dug deep into the earth.

   (C) He built railroad tracks.

   (D) He discovered hot springs there.

9. Why was the discovery of hot springs in Glenwood Canyon important?

   (A) The Ute Indians were able to settle in the area of Glenwood Canyon.

   (B) The miners were finally able to send their coal out to other communities.

   (C) The Colorado Midland Railroad was able to build tracks through the mountains.

   (D) Many people came to visit the springs, settled there, and the town of Glenwood Springs grew.

10. How did logging become an important industry in Seattle?

    (A) Airplanes are made in Seattle.

    (B) Seattle has many trees.

    (C) Chief Sealth helped the settlers.

    (D) Fish are an important resource.

11. What should loggers do to make sure that their industry continues to grow around Seattle?

    (A) plant trees to take the place of the ones they cut

    (B) continue to use the port in Seattle to ship wood

    (C) help the computer companies grow

    (D) buy airplanes that are built in Seattle

12. What happened in Indianapolis in the 1830s?

    (A) Union Rail Station was built there.

    (B) The National Road was built there.

    (C) Several highways passed through there.

    (D) Many people farmed there.

© Scott Foresman 3

13. What is one way that the businesses of Indianapolis can send their products to the rest of the country?

Ⓐ by truck on the highways leading out of the city

Ⓑ by ship on the river that runs through the city

Ⓒ by barge on the lake that is near the city

Ⓓ by ship on the ocean by which the city is located

14. Who used the Underground Railroad in Indianapolis?

Ⓐ loggers sending wood to the nearest port

Ⓑ government workers using the National Road

Ⓒ African American slaves escaping from the South to the North

Ⓓ People working in the airplane and computer industries

Part 1: Skills Test

Directions: Use complete sentences to answer questions 1–5. Use a separate sheet of paper if you need more space.

1. Suppose that Katrinka and her family move from Bozeman, Montana, to Tucson, Arizona. What will she have to do to adapt to her new environment? What activities will she have to leave behind in Bozeman? **Hypothesize**

_____

_____

_____

_____

2. How does each region's environment affect the animals that live there? Why do alligators live in the Southeast? **Make Inferences**

_____

_____

_____

_____

3. Why do you think new industries are choosing to start in Seattle? **Draw Conclusions**

_____

_____

_____

_____

4. Do you think Indianapolis will continue to be an important city in the United States? Why or why not? What might happen in its future? **Predict**

_____

_____

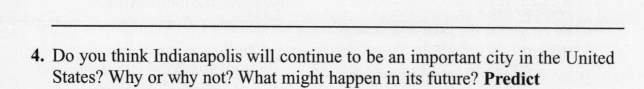

Average Monthly Snowfall in Helena, MT

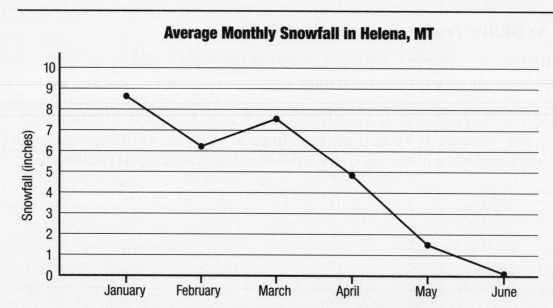

5. Use the graph to answer the questions. **Use a Line Graph**
   a. Why is reading the title of this graph important?

_____

   b. What do the numbers along the side of the graph tell?

_____

   c. How much snow falls in Helena in May?

_____

Chapter 7 Test

Part 1: Content Test

Directions: Fill in the circle next to the correct answer.

1. Europeans explored both New York and Quebec, Canada. How were those two areas similar?
   - (A) Native Americans already lived in both places.
   - (B) Both places were full of beautiful flowers.
   - (C) Explorers found golden cities in both places.
   - (D) The Iroquois farmed in both places.

2. How did the early Iroquois women use the land where they lived?
   - (A) They gathered wild berries.
   - (B) They dug pits to cook food.
   - (C) They grew crops, such as corn.
   - (D) They planted flowers.

3. What is one accomplishment shared by Columbus, De Soto, and Ponce de León?
   - (A) They all explored North America for Spain.
   - (B) They all sailed from Portugal to South America.
   - (C) They all landed in present-day Canada.
   - (D) They all competed against French explorers.

4. Which of these explorers landed in Canada?
   - (A) Hernando de Soto
   - (B) Juan Ponce de León
   - (C) Christopher Columbus
   - (D) Jacques Cartier

5. Who first gave the state of Florida its name?
   - (A) Juan Ponce de León
   - (B) Samuel de Champlain
   - (C) Christopher Columbus
   - (D) King Philip II of Spain

6. After Ponce de León left Florida, what country continued to explore there?
   - (A) Spain
   - (B) Canada
   - (C) North America
   - (D) South America

7. Who led the group that built the first permanent European settlement of St. Augustine?
   - (A) Christopher Columbus
   - (B) Jacques Cartier
   - (C) Don Pedro Menéndez de Avilés
   - (D) Samuel de Champlain

8. What European group explored both Florida and Canada?

Ⓐ French
Ⓑ Spanish
Ⓒ Portuguese
Ⓓ Dutch

9. Why did Jacques Cartier leave Canada to go back to France?

Ⓐ Menéndez and his men drove Cartier away.
Ⓑ Rapids and falls blocked his westward path to China.
Ⓒ Champlain told him to return to France.
Ⓓ He was defeated at Quebec City by the English.

10. Which present-day city is in the same place that Champlain built a settlement?

Ⓐ St. Augustine, Florida
Ⓑ Quebec City, Quebec
Ⓒ Champaign, Illinois
Ⓓ Oneida County, New York

11. How was Champlain different from Cartier?

Ⓐ Champlain was French.
Ⓑ Champlain explored Canada.
Ⓒ Champlain built a settlement.
Ⓓ Champlain found a route to China.

12. Who took 105 men on a ship from England to settle in North America?

Ⓐ Chief Powhatan
Ⓑ John Smith
Ⓒ Christopher Newport
Ⓓ Christopher Columbus

13. In which state is Jamestown located?

Ⓐ Virginia
Ⓑ Quebec
Ⓒ Florida
Ⓓ New York

14. How are the settlements of St. Augustine and Jamestown alike?

Ⓐ They are both located in the state of Florida.
Ⓑ They are both still towns in the United States.
Ⓒ They were both founded by the English.
Ⓓ They were both captured by Native Americans.

15. Why did the first English settlers come to North America?

Ⓐ to elect representatives
Ⓑ to choose their government
Ⓒ to plant crops
Ⓓ to seek their fortune

Part 2: Skills Test

Directions: Use complete sentences to answer questions 1–5. Use a separate sheet of paper if you need more space.

1. How might an Iroquois living in Oneida County feel about the arrival of the European explorers? What conflicts do you think developed? **Draw Conclusions**

_____

_____

_____

_____

2. What effects do you think Ponce de León had on the Native Americans living in Florida? **Cause and Effect**

_____

_____

_____

_____

3. How is Quebec City today like it was when it was first built? How is it different? What events in the city's history helped to change it? **Compare and Contrast**

_____

_____

_____

_____

4. Why is the history of Jamestown, Virginia, important to us today? **Draw Conclusions**

_____

_____

_____

_____

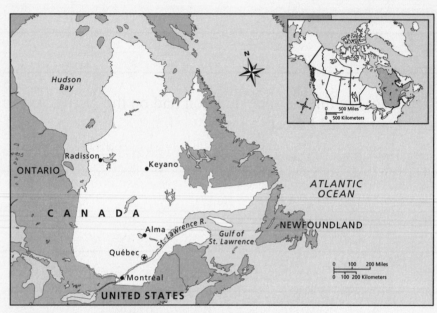

Province of Quebec, Canada

5. Use the map to answer the questions. **Use a Locator Map**
a. What area does the larger map show?

_____

b. What type of map is the smaller map? What does it show?

_____

_____

c. Where in Canada is the province of Quebec located?

_____

_____

Chapter 8 Test

Part 1: Content Test

Directions: Fill in the circle next to the correct answer.

1. What is one reason that new communities grew in the West?
   - Ⓐ Lewis and Clark told interesting stories about the West.
   - Ⓑ The trip along the Oregon Trail took six months.
   - Ⓒ People liked riding together in wagon trains.
   - Ⓓ The journey to the West was difficult and dangerous.

2. How did James Watt and Richard Trevithick help families moving west?
   - Ⓐ They opened the Transcontinental Railroad.
   - Ⓑ They guided Lewis and Clark to the Pacific Ocean.
   - Ⓒ They led wagon trains down the Oregon Trail.
   - Ⓓ They developed and improved steam engines.

3. Which inventor used a special tube to build a television?
   - Ⓐ Orville Wright
   - Ⓑ Benjamin Franklin
   - Ⓒ A. A. Campbell Swinton
   - Ⓓ Gottlieb Daimler

4. How was travel in the United States in 1917 different from travel in 1830?
   - Ⓐ In 1917 Daimler and Benz invented the first gasoline-powered car.
   - Ⓑ In 1917 there were over 250,000 more miles of railroad track than in 1830.
   - Ⓒ In 1917 most people traveled across the United States on horseback.
   - Ⓓ In 1917 many people flew on airplanes to places all over the world.

5. Which is NOT a reason why the Pony Express was set up?
   - Ⓐ People in the West wanted to communicate with the East.
   - Ⓑ Bandits often attacked wagons loaded with mail.
   - Ⓒ Many people liked to ride their horses 75 miles per day.
   - Ⓓ Weather often caused delays for the wagon trains.

© Scott Foresman 3

6. Why was mail delivered more quickly starting in 1860 than it had been before?
   (A) A group of business people set up the Pony Express.
   (B) People were able to send their letters by email.
   (C) Letters were sent on the Transcontinental Railroad.
   (D) In 1860 Samuel Morse invented the telegraph.

7. Which is NOT an accomplishment of Lewis Latimer?
   (A) He did special drawings of a telephone.
   (B) He invented a way to develop a picture.
   (C) He worked on lamps and light bulbs with Edison.
   (D) He helped many cities light their communities.

8. What did George Eastman invent in 1888?
   (A) He invented a camera that anyone could use to take a picture.
   (B) He invented a type of picture that appeared on a piece of metal.
   (C) He invented a sharp blade with a long handle for harvesting crops.
   (D) He invented a way to light factories and homes.

9. Why is Louis Pasteur an important scientist to people around the world?
   (A) He made milk safe for people to drink.
   (B) He invented a way to light people's homes.
   (C) He helped people fight off smallpox.
   (D) He created many types of machines.

10. Why is Jonas Salk's polio vaccine important?
    (A) The vaccine harms a person's healthy cells.
    (B) The vaccine destroys a person's spinal cord.
    (C) The vaccine did not work.
    (D) The vaccine saved the lives of many people.

11. Which is NOT an accomplishment of Gertrude Elion?
    (A) She helped treat people who had leukemia and malaria.
    (B) She developed a way to kill off certain germs in milk.
    (C) She figured out how to make medicine to attack diseased cells.
    (D) She won a Nobel Prize for her work in medicine.

© Scott Foresman 3

12. What did Cyrus Hall McCormick invent to make farming easier?

   Ⓐ horse

   Ⓑ lamp

   Ⓒ camera

   Ⓓ reaper

13. Who found a way to protect people from smallpox?

   Ⓐ Edward Jenner

   Ⓑ Louis Pasteur

   Ⓒ Gertrude Elion

   Ⓓ Jonas Salk

Part 2: Skills Test

Directions: Use complete sentences to answer questions 1–4. Use a separate sheet of paper if you need more space.

1. What effect did improvements in transportation have on communities in the United States? Give specific examples. **Cause and Effect**

_____

_____

_____

_____

2. What might have happened had the Transcontinental Railroad not been built? **Hypothesize**

_____

_____

3. What are at least three details to support this main idea? **The invention of the light bulb changed the way people lived. Main Idea and Details**

_____

_____

_____

4. Which of the inventions from this chapter, such as the car, the telegraph, the light bulb, or the polio vaccine, do you think is the most important? Why? **Express Ideas**

_____

_____

_____

_____

Communication Over Time

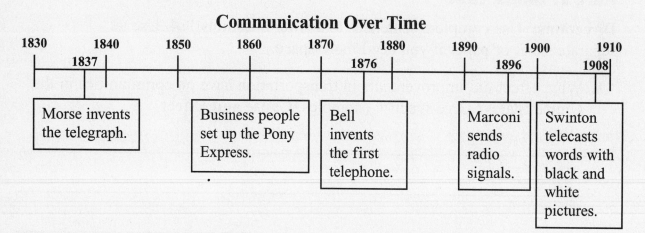

5. Use the time line to answer the questions. **Use a Time Line**
   a. What years does the time line cover?

   _____

   b. How long after Marconi sent radio signals were the first black and white pictures telecast?

   _____

   c. Which event happened first: the invention of the telegraph or the invention of the telephone? How do you know?

   _____

   _____

   _____

Unit 4 Test

Part 1: Content Test

Directions: Fill in the circle next to the correct answer.

1. How did the Iroquois obtain much of their food, such as corn?

   (A) The women were farmers.

   (B) The men were hunters.

   (C) The women were gatherers.

   (D) The men were farmers.

2. Whom did the French, Spanish, and English all meet when they arrived in North America?

   (A) Ponce de León

   (B) Dutch settlers

   (C) Native Americans

   (D) Chief Powhatan

3. Which of these explorers did NOT build a settlement in North America?

   (A) Christopher Columbus

   (B) Samuel de Champlain

   (C) Hernando de Soto

   (D) Jacques Cartier

4. Where did Ponce de León first land and explore?

   (A) in South America

   (B) north of present-day St. Augustine, Florida

   (C) near Quebec City, Quebec

   (D) east of Jamestown, Virginia

5. What was the result of Jacques Cartier's exploration of Canada?

   (A) He built a settlement that is today a Canadian city.

   (B) He stayed at a castlelike hotel overlooking the St. Lawrence River.

   (C) He realized that there was no direct route to China.

   (D) He entertained people throughout Canada with his juggling act.

6. What settlement did Christopher Newport and the others who came with him build?

   (A) St. Augustine

   (B) Jamestown

   (C) Quebec City

   (D) Newfoundland

7. Who told stories that made people want to move west in search of a better life?

   (A) Sacagawea and Powhatan

   (B) Lewis and Clark

   (C) Menéndez and Columbus

   (D) Cartier and Champlain

8. What allowed people to travel on new roads and highways across America after 1903?

Ⓐ the airplane
Ⓑ the Transcontinental Railroad
Ⓒ the Oregon Trail
Ⓓ the automobile

9. Why was it important to Americans in the late 1700s that Benjamin Franklin set up post offices?

Ⓐ The Pony Express needed places for the riders and horses to rest.
Ⓑ In the 1800s people needed a better way to get a letter to families and friends.
Ⓒ Benjamin Franklin wanted to meet people all over the country.
Ⓓ Americans needed a place to pick up their mail after it arrived by train.

10. How did the reaper help farmers of the 1800s?
Ⓐ Farming was made easier with a machine and a horse.
Ⓑ Farmers were able to take pictures of their fields.
Ⓒ Farmers could communicate quickly with others.
Ⓓ Farmers could walk through and harvest a field.

11. How did Samuel Morse help Americans communicate faster?

Ⓐ He developed a way for people to be able to handwrite letters more quickly to family and friends.
Ⓑ His invention of email allowed people to use their computers to send messages around the world.
Ⓒ He set up the Pony Express, which delivered letters across the country more quickly than by wagon train.
Ⓓ He invented the telegraph, which could send messages across the country in just seconds.

12. How did Louis Daguerre change the way people remembered their favorite times?

Ⓐ He made drawings of a type of telephone.
Ⓑ He invented the light bulb and electric lamps.
Ⓒ He invented the reaper.
Ⓓ He invented a way to develop pictures.

13. How does pasteurization help make milk safe to drink?

Ⓐ Milk is heated to the point that certain germs are killed.
Ⓑ Milk is injected with a very weak form of smallpox.
Ⓒ Milk is heated and mixed with the polio vaccine.
Ⓓ Milk is used to attack diseased cells.

Part 2: Skills Test

Directions: Use complete sentences to answer questions 1–3. Use a separate sheet of paper if you need more space.

1. How did the relationship between Juan Ponce de León and the Native Americans affect Spanish settlements in the area? **Express Ideas**

   _____

   _____

   _____

   _____

2. What are the major types of transportation that have been used in the United States? Write key events in the history of transportation in the order they happened. **Sequence**

   _____

   _____

   _____

   _____

3. What effect have vaccinations had on the lives of people today? **Cause and Effect**

   _____

   _____

   _____

   _____

   _____

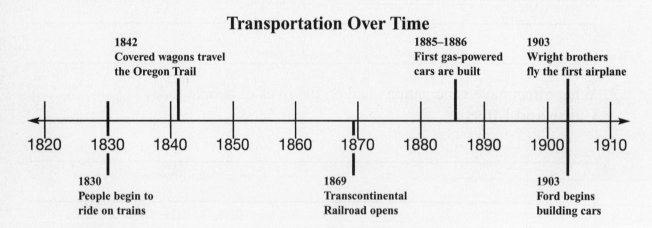

Florida

4. Use the map to answer the questions. **Use a Locator Map**
   a. What area does the locator map show? _____

   b. What does the box on the locator map show?

   _____

   c. Why does the larger map show some major cities, but the smaller map does not?

   _____

   _____

Transportation Over Time

1842
Covered wagons travel
the Oregon Trail

1885–1886
First gas-powered
cars are built

1903
Wright brothers
fly the first airplane

1820   1830   1840   1850   1860   1870   1880   1890   1900   1910

1830
People begin to
ride on trains

1869
Transcontinental
Railroad opens

1903
Ford begins
building cars

5. Use the time line to answer the questions. **Use a Time Line**
   a. How many years are shown on the time line? _____

   b. When did the Transcontinental Railroad open? _____

   c. Construction of the Lincoln Highway began in 1913. Why isn't that event shown on this time line? _____

Name _____ Date _____

Chapter 9 Test

Part 1: Content Test

Directions: Fill in the circle next to the correct answer.

1. Which is a way to earn money?
   - Ⓐ walk your neighbor's dog
   - Ⓑ buy a new softball bat
   - Ⓒ save money in a bank
   - Ⓓ buy two CDs for $20

2. Which is NOT a way to spend money?
   - Ⓐ buy your own lunch in your school cafeteria
   - Ⓑ give your brother $10 for his birthday
   - Ⓒ run errands for your older neighbors
   - Ⓓ donate $5 a week to your church offering

3. Which three columns are important to have on a budget?
   - Ⓐ Wants, Needs, and Supplies
   - Ⓑ Income, Spending, and Saving
   - Ⓒ Softballs, Bats, and Gloves
   - Ⓓ Week 1, Week 2, and Week 3

4. What is a *need*?
   - Ⓐ A need is something you would like but can live without.
   - Ⓑ A need is a plan that shows income, spending, and saving.
   - Ⓒ A need is the amount of money a person uses each day.
   - Ⓓ A need is something that a person must have to live.

5. Which of the following is an example of a *want*?
   - Ⓐ a softball bat
   - Ⓑ fresh water
   - Ⓒ food to eat
   - Ⓓ a place to live

6. Which is an example of an economic choice?
   - Ⓐ Robin chooses to buy a softball bat instead of two CDs.
   - Ⓑ Robin chooses to sit by her sister at lunch instead of by her friends.
   - Ⓒ Robin chooses to play softball instead of basketball.
   - Ⓓ Robin chooses to eat chicken nuggets instead of a hamburger at lunch.

© Scott Foresman 3

7. Why did Robin make a chart about softball bats?
   Ⓐ to give to the owner of the sporting goods store
   Ⓑ to help her decide which one she should buy
   Ⓒ to show her father how to make a chart
   Ⓓ to prepare for her test on softball bats

8. What was Robin's opportunity cost when she bought the softball bat?
   Ⓐ a softball
   Ⓑ ten bats
   Ⓒ two CDs
   Ⓓ a T-ball bat

9. Suppose that your mother buys a pair of shoes instead of a jacket. What is her opportunity cost?
   Ⓐ the pair of shoes
   Ⓑ a pair of socks
   Ⓒ the jacket
   Ⓓ two CDs

10. Which is a good that a sporting goods store might sell?
    Ⓐ a softball bat
    Ⓑ baseball lessons
    Ⓒ umpire for games
    Ⓓ people to sew uniforms

11. What usually happens when the supply of a product goes up?
    Ⓐ The price of that product also goes up.
    Ⓑ The demand for that product also goes up.
    Ⓒ The producers of that product make more of it.
    Ⓓ The price of that product goes down.

12. What might a store owner do if few people are buying a certain product?
    Ⓐ The store owner might open a new store for the product.
    Ⓑ The store owner might raise the price of the product.
    Ⓒ The store owner might lower the price of the product.
    Ⓓ The store owner might order more of the product.

13. What is *profit*?
    Ⓐ the income a business has left after all its costs are paid
    Ⓑ the money that a business spends over the course of a year
    Ⓒ the amount of a product that people want and can pay for
    Ⓓ the amount of money a business brings in

14. What must a business do in order to make a profit?
    (A) It has to spend more money than it is able to save.
    (B) It has to supply more products than people demand.
    (C) It has to sell a product for more than the cost to make it.
    (D) It has to provide a service to the community.

15. What is one thing that a store owner can do to increase profit?
    (A) sell goods at a lower price
    (B) provide services for free
    (C) increase the supply of goods
    (D) sell goods at a higher price

Part 2: Skills Test

Directions: Use complete sentences to answer questions 1–5. Use a separate sheet of paper if you need more space.

1. Suppose you want to buy a new keyboard, but you need to save for the purchase. Describe, in the order in which they happen, the events involved in creating and using a budget to save for the keyboard. **Sequence**

_____

_____

_____

_____

_____

2. Think about your last trip to the grocery store or mall. What did you or your family buy? Which items were needs and which items were wants? **Categorize**

_____

_____

_____

_____

3. Suppose that your school principal has $5,000 to spend. She could buy new computers, new books for the library, or new playground equipment. Which do you think she should buy? Why? **Apply Information**

_____

_____

_____

_____

_____

4. Suppose that you earned $25 for walking a neighbor's dog last month. Will you spend the money or save it? If you spend some of it, what will you buy? What steps will you take in deciding what to do with your money? Write the steps in the order in which they will happen. **Sequence**

_____

_____

_____

_____

_____

5. Suppose a store in your community sells only soccer equipment. What might happen to the store if community interest in soccer decreases? Why? What can the store owner do to solve this problem? **Cause and Effect**

_____

_____

_____

_____

_____

_____

Chapter 10 Test

Part 1: Content Test

Directions: Fill in the circle next to the correct answer.

1. Which natural resource is used to make a softball bat?
   - (A) fish
   - (B) trees
   - (C) coal
   - (D) oil

2. Which is NOT a capital resource?
   - (A) a building where bats are made
   - (B) a computer that runs a machine
   - (C) a worker who shapes bats by hand
   - (D) a machine that cuts softball bats

3. How can computerized machines help a business make greater profits?
   - (A) The machines are expensive and cost the company a lot of money.
   - (B) The company can track its spending on the computer.
   - (C) Making products more quickly can cost the company less money.
   - (D) Machines can make people buy more of the company's product.

4. What must happen before a worker can sand a piece of wood to make a softball bat?
   - (A) A worker must dip the bat into colored paint.
   - (B) Someone must go to the store and buy the softball bat.
   - (C) A computerized machine must sand the piece of wood.
   - (D) A tree must be cut down and split into lumber.

5. What does it mean to say a resource is "scarce"?
   - (A) There is too much of it.
   - (B) There is not enough of it.
   - (C) There is a lot of it.
   - (D) There is none of it.

6. Which of these is NOT a resource that is scarce?
   - (A) wood
   - (B) gasoline
   - (C) coal
   - (D) sunshine

7. What might happen if a community chooses to use wood to build a new playground?
   - (A) There might not be enough wood for something else.
   - (B) Many new trees might grow on the playground.
   - (C) There might not be enough gasoline to power people's cars.
   - (D) The lumber company might not make enough profit.

8. For which resource does Phoenix, Arizona, have to depend on Portland, Oregon?
   - (A) water
   - (B) wood
   - (C) coal
   - (D) oil

9. What happens before lumber is delivered to a community?
   - (A) A community builds a fence.
   - (B) Furniture is made from the lumber.
   - (C) A driver unloads the lumber.
   - (D) Trees are cut down and milled.

10. Who provides a service that allows lumber to get to cities around the country?
    - (A) truck driver
    - (B) bat maker
    - (C) umpire
    - (D) letter carrier

11. Which is NOT a reason why people trade with each other?
    - (A) to get goods they cannot make
    - (B) to make money from the trade
    - (C) to benefit from the trade
    - (D) to travel and meet new people

12. What is *communication*?
    - (A) sharing of information or news
    - (B) buying of goods and services
    - (C) trading between two countries
    - (D) sending of goods to a country

13. Which of the following is one way goods were transported during ancient times and today?
    - (A) by train
    - (B) by truck
    - (C) by ship
    - (D) by airplane

14. What is a *free market*?
    - (A) a market in which the government tells you what to produce and buy
    - (B) a market in which people choose what to produce and buy
    - (C) a market that trades goods with another country
    - (D) a market that gives all of its products away for free

© Scott Foresman 3

Part 2: Skills Test

Directions: Use complete sentences to answer questions 1–4. Use a separate sheet of paper if you need more space.

1. What natural resources do you use at school? What human resources and capital resources do you use? **Categorize**

   _____

   _____

   _____

   _____

2. Suppose you are the leader of Robin's community. What steps would you have to take in deciding what to do with your community's land? Write those steps in the order in which they would occur. **Sequence**

   _____

   _____

   _____

   _____

3. What are three examples to support the following main idea? **In the United States, people and companies are part of a free market. Main Idea and Details**

   _____

   _____

   _____

© Scott Foresman 3

4. Often when countries disagree, they refuse to trade with each other. What effect might such disagreements have on the people who live in those countries? **Cause and Effect**

_____

_____

_____

_____

_____

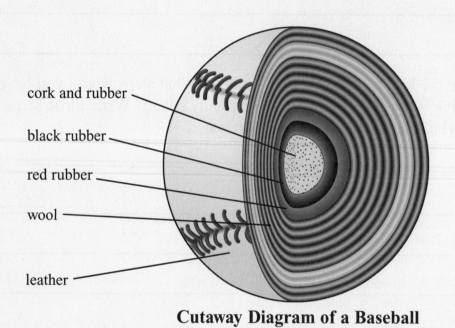

cork and rubber

black rubber

red rubber

wool

leather

Cutaway Diagram of a Baseball

5. Use the diagram to answer the questions. **Use a Cutaway Diagram**
   a. What does the diagram show?

   _____

   b. What is the outer layer of the ball made from? _____

   c. What is between the black rubber layer and the wool layer?

   _____

Unit 5 Test

Part 1: Content Test

Directions: Fill in the circle next to the correct answer.

1. Which is NOT something that would be found on a budget?
   - (A) the amount of money you saved last week
   - (B) the amount of money you earned babysitting
   - (C) the amount of money you spent on a gift
   - (D) the amount of money you want to spend on a new bat

2. How does a want differ from a need?
   - (A) A want is something you would like to have but can live without.
   - (B) A want is something made of wood, such as a softball bat.
   - (C) A want is something that you must have in order to live.
   - (D) A want is something made from a nonrenewable resource.

3. Which is NOT an example of an economic choice?
   - (A) Your school buys computers instead of science equipment.
   - (B) Your mother buys a loaf of bread instead of rolls.
   - (C) Your sister wears her red boots instead of her tennis shoes.
   - (D) Your community builds a playground instead of a swimming pool.

4. What is an opportunity cost?
   - (A) something you would like to have but can live without
   - (B) what you give up when you choose one thing instead of another
   - (C) a plan to help you track your earning and spending
   - (D) when you buy one thing instead of another

5. What might happen if the demand for a product were to go up?
   - (A) The production of that product might stop.
   - (B) The supply of that product might stay the same.
   - (C) The price of that product might go down.
   - (D) The price of that product might go up.

6. Which is NOT an example of a human resource?
   - (A) a computer that cuts bats
   - (B) a woman who sands bats
   - (C) a man who umpires a game
   - (D) an employee of a sporting goods store

7. What might happen if a softball bat maker has to increase pay for its workers?
   A The bat maker probably will have a sale on softball bats.
   B Unless it also charges its customers more, it will lose some of its profits.
   C The owner might have to give the bats to customers for free.
   D Because of the price of making bats, it will make only balls.

8. Why is Portland, Oregon, important to Phoenix, Arizona?
   A Because there are so many trees in Arizona, communities there send their logs to mills in Portland.
   B Because trees are scarce, communities in Arizona build products out of metal and sell them in Portland.
   C Because trees are scarce, communities in Arizona must get their lumber from places such as Portland.
   D Because there are so many trees in Arizona, communities there share their lumber with Portland.

9. How has communication helped increase trade?
   A If a grocery store needs goods quickly, it can email its suppliers.
   B People can now move goods quickly around the world.
   C Today people often trade goods and services for money.
   D People now can buy and sell services.

10. Which is NOT a reason why people trade with each other?
    A to get something they can already make for themselves
    B to make money from selling their goods and services
    C to get something they cannot make or grow for themselves
    D to find goods they can use in making other goods

11. How is the market in some other countries different from the market in the United States?
    A In other countries people choose what to produce.
    B In other countries people choose what to buy.
    C In some countries the government decides what is bought and sold.
    D In other countries people and companies are a part of a free market.

Part 2: Skills Test

Directions: Use complete sentences to answer questions 1–4. Use a separate sheet of paper if you need more space.

1. Think of a large purchase you would like to make. What steps should you take before buying that item? Write, in the order in which they happen, the steps to creating a budget and making an economic choice. **Sequence**

_____

_____

_____

2. Suppose a business were to pay its workers less money than it had in the past. How might it affect other businesses in the community? **Cause and Effect**

_____

_____

_____

3. Why is it important to use natural resources wisely? Human and capital resources? How might human and capital resources be used wisely? **Make Inferences**

_____

_____

_____

_____

_____

4. Would you like to live in a country that does not have a free market? Why or why not? **Make Decisions**

_____

_____

_____

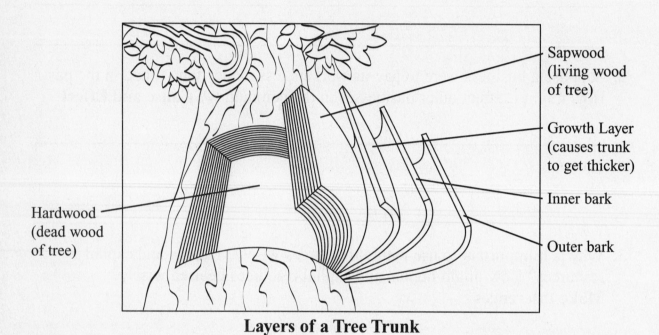

Layers of a Tree Trunk

5. Use the diagram to answer the questions. **Use a Cutaway Diagram**
  a. What is the outer layer of a tree trunk called?

_____

  b. What part causes the tree trunk to get thicker?

_____

  c. Baseball bats are made from the hardwood of a tree. Where in the trunk is that layer found?

_____

Chapter 11 Test

Part 1: Content Test

Directions: Fill in the circle next to the correct answer.

1. Which is NOT a reason why the people of ancient Greece formed a community?
   - Ⓐ to have a safe place to work
   - Ⓑ to have a safe place to live
   - Ⓒ to live under a set of fair laws
   - Ⓓ to form a republic

2. What is one way government buildings in Washington, D.C., compare with those in ancient Greece?
   - Ⓐ Both were built on the water.
   - Ⓑ Both look like small houses.
   - Ⓒ Both have a similar style of architecture.
   - Ⓓ Both lack a roof.

3. How does the government of ancient Greece differ from the U.S. government?
   - Ⓐ Both countries are run by kings.
   - Ⓑ Greece had a direct democracy; the United States has a republic.
   - Ⓒ Greece had a republic; the United States has a direct democracy.
   - Ⓓ Greece had no form of government, but the United States does.

4. Where can many of the ideas from the Magna Carta be found today?
   - Ⓐ in the U.S. Constitution
   - Ⓑ in the Mayflower Compact
   - Ⓒ in the home of King John
   - Ⓓ in Greek laws

5. What did the Mayflower Compact say?
   - Ⓐ Only the King of England could make laws.
   - Ⓑ The colonists themselves would make laws.
   - Ⓒ The Magna Carta would no longer be in effect.
   - Ⓓ The people of Athens could live in a republic.

6. What did the Declaration of Independence say?
   - Ⓐ The government of England was always right and fair.
   - Ⓑ The colonists would all go back to live in England.
   - Ⓒ The Mayflower Compact could not be used in the colonies.
   - Ⓓ The colonies were free and no longer part of England.

7. Which is NOT true about the U.S. Constitution?
   Ⓐ It was a plan for our government.
   Ⓑ James Madison helped write it.
   Ⓒ King John agreed with its ideas.
   Ⓓ It gives the power to the people.

8. Who was chosen to make plans for Washington, D.C.?
   Ⓐ George Washington
   Ⓑ Pierre Charles L'Enfant
   Ⓒ Thomas Jefferson
   Ⓓ Thurgood Marshall

9. What is included in the Bill of Rights?
   Ⓐ protection of the people's rights
   Ⓑ fifteen amendments to the Constitution
   Ⓒ the declaration of independence from England
   Ⓓ the point of view of the king of England

10. How did Rosa Parks help change her community?
    Ⓐ She believed that all people's rights should be protected and, in time, they were.
    Ⓑ She liked to ride the bus to work, and she encouraged others to ride it too.
    Ⓒ She sewed new clothes for every person who lived in her community.
    Ⓓ She was the first member of her community to serve on the U.S. Supreme Court.

11. How do you know that Rosa Parks and Thurgood Marshall were good citizens?
    Ⓐ They both refused to give up a seat on the bus.
    Ⓑ They both lived and worked in Washington, D.C.
    Ⓒ They both rode the bus to work each day.
    Ⓓ They both showed a belief in equality and justice.

12. Which is NOT a responsibility of a good citizen?

Ⓐ obeying laws

Ⓑ voting in elections

Ⓒ running for office

Ⓓ paying taxes

13. What should a good citizen do after an election?

Ⓐ A good citizen should be angry if his or her favorite candidate lost.

Ⓑ A good citizen should accept the results of the election.

Ⓒ A good citizen should count all the votes that were cast.

Ⓓ A good citizen should work to defeat the new leader in the next election.

14. How can you help decide how your student government is run?

Ⓐ vote in city elections

Ⓑ vote in county elections

Ⓒ complain to other students

Ⓓ vote in school elections

15. What is something you can do to improve your community?

Ⓐ You can volunteer to help people who are hungry.

Ⓑ You can throw trash and food in the streets.

Ⓒ You can obey only those laws that you think are fair.

Ⓓ You cannot personally do anything to improve a community.

Part 2: Skills Test

Directions: Use complete sentences to answer questions 1–5. Use a separate sheet of paper if you need more space.

1. How is a direct democracy like a republic? How is it different? **Compare and Contrast**

_____

_____

_____

_____

2. What are five documents that are important to our country's history? List them in the order in which they were written. **Sequence**

_____

_____

_____

_____

3. What was Thomas Jefferson's point of view about England? How do you know? **Summarize**

_____

_____

_____

_____

4. Suppose that a summary you are writing has the following main idea: **Rosa Parks and Thurgood Marshall were good citizens.** What details would you include in your summary? **Main Idea and Details**

_____

_____

_____

_____

5. What are three things that you can do to make your community a better place in which to live? **Apply Information**

_____

_____

_____

_____

Chapter 12 Test

Part 1: Content Test

Directions: Fill in the circle next to the correct answer.

1. Which is NOT one of the services people expect from their government?
   Ⓐ education
   Ⓑ transportation
   Ⓒ communication
   Ⓓ recreation

2. How can a local government meet people's need for safety?
   Ⓐ by building a nature center
   Ⓑ by operating a police department
   Ⓒ by planting trees in the community
   Ⓓ by forming a city or town council

3. Which of the following is an educational service provided by many local governments?
   Ⓐ police departments
   Ⓑ sports leagues
   Ⓒ libraries
   Ⓓ senior centers

4. Which is NOT a form of recreation provided by local governments?
   Ⓐ parks
   Ⓑ swimming pools
   Ⓒ schools
   Ⓓ senior centers

5. How can a local government make transportation easier for its citizens?
   Ⓐ by building a swimming pool
   Ⓑ by adding books to the library
   Ⓒ by building and fixing roads
   Ⓓ by picking up citizens' trash

6. What is one way local governments get money to pay for the services they provide?
   Ⓐ They charge fees for some services.
   Ⓑ They invest in the stock market.
   Ⓒ They ask for donations.
   Ⓓ They do not pay for the services they provide.

7. How are the members of a town or city council chosen?
   Ⓐ Adults in the community vote.
   Ⓑ The mayor chooses them.
   Ⓒ The school board chooses them.
   Ⓓ People take a test to become members.

8. Which of the following can veto a bill?
   Ⓐ mayor
   Ⓑ chief
   Ⓒ police officer
   Ⓓ governor

9. Which is NOT usually a job of the mayor and the city council?
   (A) deciding what they want the local government to do
   (B) picking people to provide services
   (C) choosing the police chief and the fire chief
   (D) running the police department and the fire department

10. How are community leaders able to make and carry out laws?
    (A) Candidates read books about carrying out laws.
    (B) The mayor demands that citizens obey laws.
    (C) The leaders take a class about making laws.
    (D) People give their consent to the leaders.

11. What happens if an elected leader does not do a good job?
    (A) The people may not vote for that person in the next election.
    (B) The person must give his or her position to someone else.
    (C) The person must serve on the town council for two more years.
    (D) The people may elect that person mayor at the next election.

12. After a governor vetoes a bill, what might happen?
    (A) the bill becomes law
    (B) the Legislative branch votes on the bill again
    (C) the bill goes to another branch of government
    (D) the governor rewrites the bill

13. What is one way a person can improve his or her community?
    (A) by disobeying the laws of the community
    (B) by never voting in community elections
    (C) by picking up trash in the community
    (D) by driving fast on busy streets in the community

14. What two groups of lawmakers make up most state Legislatures?
    (A) the House of Representatives and the Senate
    (B) the Judicial branch and the Executive branch
    (C) the Senate and the governor
    (D) Judges and juries

Part 2: Skills Test

Directions: Use complete sentences to answer questions 1–4. Use a separate sheet of paper if you need more space.

1. Suppose that you are writing a summary about the services that local governments provide. What is your summary's main idea? What is one detail from your summary? **Summarize**

   _____

   _____

   _____

   _____

2. When you are older, you probably will have to pay taxes to your local government. How do you feel about taxes? Are they important? Should every citizen have to pay them? Why or why not? **Express Ideas**

   _____

   _____

   _____

   _____

3. Name at least three offices in local government. Tell whether each position is elected or chosen. **Categorize**

   _____

   _____

   _____

   _____

4. Would you like to work for your local government when you are older? Why or why not? What position would you like to hold? **Apply Information**

_____

_____

_____

_____

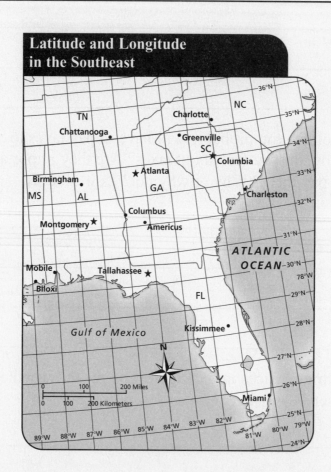

Latitude and Longitude in the Southeast

5. Use the map to fill in the blank boxes of the table.
Understand Latitude and Longitude

Closest Latitude and Longitude on Map	Closest City
	Charlotte
34°N, 81°W	
26°N, 80°W	
	Americus

Unit 6 Test

Part 1: Content Test

Directions: Fill in the circle next to the correct answer.

1. Where did architects in Washington, D.C., get many of their ideas for designing government buildings?
   - (A) from the Magna Carta
   - (B) from the Mayflower Compact
   - (C) from stories about ancient Greece
   - (D) from buildings in ancient Greece

2. How did the citizens of ancient Athens know that their community would have fair laws?
   - (A) The citizens created their own laws.
   - (B) The citizens elected fair officials to create laws.
   - (C) The citizens knew that their king would make fair laws.
   - (D) The citizens lived under the rules of the Magna Carta.

3. Which two documents influenced the founders of our country?
   - (A) the Mayflower Compact and the *Mayflower*
   - (B) the Mayflower Compact and ancient Greece
   - (C) the Magna Carta and a letter from King John
   - (D) the Magna Carta and the Mayflower Compact

4. Which is NOT a document important to the United States?
   - (A) Bill of Rights
   - (B) U.S. Constitution
   - (C) U.S. Capitol
   - (D) Declaration of Independence

5. What did Pierre Charles L'Enfant do?
   - (A) He made the plans for Washington, D.C.
   - (B) He built the U.S. Capitol building by hand.
   - (C) He was the first President of our country.
   - (D) He helped Jefferson with the Bill of Rights.

6. How was Rosa Parks different from Thurgood Marshall?
   - (A) Rosa Parks believed in equality and justice.
   - (B) Rosa Parks was a good citizen of her community.
   - (C) Rosa Parks helped change our country.
   - (D) Rosa Parks refused to give up her seat on a bus.

7. How should every good citizen help his or her elected leaders?
   (A) by obeying the laws that leaders pass
   (B) by working on a leader's staff
   (C) by giving all of his or her money to the leaders
   (D) by running for office

8. Which is a responsibility of a good citizen?
   (A) deciding what property others may keep
   (B) disobeying laws
   (C) voting in elections
   (D) running for office

9. Which is NOT a kind of service that local governments often provide to citizens?
   (A) education
   (B) transportation
   (C) communication
   (D) recreation

10. How might your family help your local government pay for the services it provides?
    (A) by buying a traffic signal
    (B) by paying for trash pickup
    (C) by connecting to the Internet
    (D) by refusing to pay taxes

11. How can a student help improve his or her school?
    (A) try to use as many school supplies as possible
    (B) refuse to obey his or her teacher and principal
    (C) vote for leaders to run the student government
    (D) attend his or her classes regularly

12. How are city council members usually chosen?
    (A) Candidates take a social studies test.
    (B) The police chief chooses council members.
    (C) Adults in a community vote for local leaders.
    (D) Local teachers decide who is the smartest.

13. How do voters give their consent to their leaders?
    (A) by running behind their leaders
    (B) by cheering for their leaders
    (C) by writing their leaders a letter
    (D) by electing their leaders to office

Part 2: Skills Test

Directions: Use complete sentences to answer questions 1–4. Use a separate sheet of paper if you need more space.

1. Why do you think other countries have used our Constitution as a guide when setting up their governments? **Make Inferences**

_____

_____

_____

_____

_____

2. Suppose that you are writing a summary about being a good citizen. What is your main idea? What is one detail from your summary? **Summarize**

_____

_____

_____

3. What services does your local government provide for its citizens? Tell whether each is an education, recreation, transportation, or safety service. **Categorize**

_____

_____

_____

_____

4. Suppose that while playing at a city park, you notice that the playground is unsafe. How can you help solve this problem? **Solve Problems**

_____

_____

_____

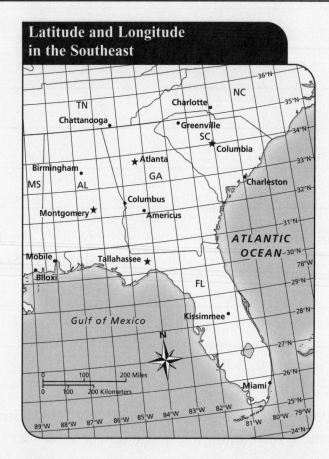

Latitude and Longitude in the Southeast

5. Use the map to answer the questions. **Understand Latitude and Longitude**
   a. Which directions do lines of latitude run? Which directions do lines of longitude run?

_____

_____

   b. Which line of latitude forms the northern boundary of Alabama and Georgia? _____

   c. Which city is closest to 31°N, 88°W? _____

Chapter 1 Test

Part 1: Content Test

Directions: Fill in the circle next to the correct answer.

Lesson Objective (1:1)

1. What is a community?
   - ● where people live, work, and have fun together
   - Ⓑ where people visit on vacation
   - Ⓒ where people go to work
   - Ⓓ where people cross a bridge over the Rio Grande

Lesson Objective (1:3)

2. Which sentence tells something about the history of El Paso, Texas?
   - ● It was first settled by Native Americans and then by the Spanish.
   - Ⓑ People work and have fun together in El Paso.
   - Ⓒ El Paso is Spanish and means "the pass."
   - Ⓓ Carlos lives in the community of El Paso, Texas.

Lesson Objective (1:2)

3. Where is the community of El Paso, Texas, located?
   - Ⓐ near beautiful lakes
   - ● between two sets of mountains
   - Ⓒ where two rivers meet
   - Ⓓ in a desert region

Lesson Objective (1:4)

4. Which detail supports the following main idea? **There are many fun things to do and see in El Paso.**
   - ● From Rim Road you can see into Mexico for miles.
   - Ⓑ Carlos's parents vote for people who want to help the community.
   - Ⓒ Letter carriers deliver the mail in El Paso.
   - Ⓓ El Paso is more than 400 years old.

Lesson Objective (2:2)

5. In which state is Astoria located?
   - Ⓐ Colorado
   - Ⓑ Texas
   - Ⓒ North Carolina
   - ● Oregon

Lesson Objective (2:4)

6. Which main idea does the following detail support? **Farming communities are located in areas with rich soil.**
   - Ⓐ Anna lives in Astoria.
   - Ⓑ Astoria is almost 200 years old.
   - Ⓒ Anna's cousins live in Denver.
   - ● Communities are located in special places.

Lesson Objective (2:4)

7. Which detail supports the following main idea? **The Pacific Ocean is important to the community of Astoria.**
   - Ⓐ Astoria has many historical museums to visit.
   - Ⓑ Astoria is on the other side of the United States from Wilmington.
   - ● People in Astoria like to fish, swim, boat, and ride the waves.
   - Ⓓ Astoria holds a special celebration in June.

Lesson Objective (2:3)

8. How would you best describe the area where Wilmington is located?
   - ● It is between the Cape Fear River and the Atlantic Ocean.
   - Ⓑ It was first settled by Native Americans.
   - Ⓒ It is where Anna's grandparents live.
   - Ⓓ It is a dot on a map.

Lesson Objective (2:3)

9. Who settled in Wilmington after the Native Americans?
   - ● English
   - Ⓑ Arapaho
   - Ⓒ Texans
   - Ⓓ Norwegians

Lesson Objective (2:1)

10. How are Denver, Colorado, and Wilmington, North Carolina, alike?
    - Ⓐ They are both located in the Rocky Mountains.
    - ● They both were settled by Native Americans.
    - Ⓒ They are both near Bald Head Island.
    - Ⓓ Gold brought prospectors to both communities.

Lesson Objective (3:1)

11. What are some things that culture includes?
    - Ⓐ computers and textbooks
    - Ⓑ parks, stores, and hospitals
    - ● language, food, and holidays
    - Ⓓ mountains, rivers, and oceans

Lesson Objective (3:1)

12. Which of these describes a part of the culture of Timbuktu, Mali?
    - Ⓐ Mali is located in West Africa.
    - Ⓑ Merchants once did lots of business in Timbuktu.
    - ● The main language in Mali is French.
    - Ⓓ The sun shines brightly almost every day in Mali.

Lesson Objective (3:2)

13. How is Timbuktu today like it was in the past?
    - ● Religion is still very important to the people of Timbuktu.
    - Ⓑ Today many thousands of people live in Timbuktu.
    - Ⓒ Timbuktu is still a center of learning.
    - Ⓓ Camels carry blocks of salt to and from the city.

Lesson Objective (3:3)

14. What might you have seen in Timbuktu four to six centuries ago?
    - ● camels carrying goods on their backs
    - Ⓑ the only two mosques in the city
    - Ⓒ fewer people than you see today
    - Ⓓ rain falling every day

Part 2: Skills Test

Directions: Use complete sentences to answer questions 1–4. Use a separate sheet of paper if you need more space.

1. Give three details to support the following main idea: **Many people work together to make El Paso a special community. Main Idea and Details**

   Possible answers should include three of the following:
   teachers, letter carriers, police officers, doctors, people work in stores, people go to community meetings, and they vote for people who want to help others in the community.

2. Describe the area where your community is located. How might its location help it grow in the future? **Predict**

   Answers should reflect an understanding of the geography of the students' community and the role that geography and location play in its history.

3. How did Denver first begin? How did it grow? Write the events of Denver's history in order. **Sequence**

   Denver began as a Native American Arapaho settlement.
   Then the fur traders, miners and prospectors arrived.

4. Suppose that you are to take a trip to Timbuktu, Mali. What is the weather like there? What should you plan to take with you? **Solve Problems**

   Mali is located in a desert region. Very little rain falls there.
   The sun shines every day. Students might take sunglasses,
   a hat, sunscreen, and lightweight clothes.

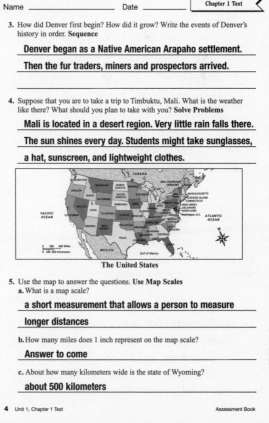

The United States

5. Use the map to answer the questions. **Use Map Scales**
   a. What is a map scale?

   a short measurement that allows a person to measure longer distances

   b. How many miles does 1 inch represent on the map scale?

   Answer to come

   c. About how many kilometers wide is the state of Wyoming?

   about 500 kilometers

Chapter 2 Test

Part 1: Content Test

Directions: Fill in the circle next to the correct answer.

Lesson Objective (1:1)

1. How would you describe a rural community?
   - ● The towns are small and far apart.
   - Ⓑ The towns are very big.
   - Ⓒ The towns have many people living in them.
   - Ⓓ There are no towns in a rural community.

Lesson Objective (1:1)

2. What are rural communities usually surrounded by?
   - Ⓐ many houses
   - ● open lands and fields
   - Ⓒ deserts and mountains
   - Ⓓ water

Lesson Objective (1:3)

3. How would you describe the area where Bridgewater is located?
   - Ⓐ It is located between two sets of mountains.
   - Ⓑ It is located in the Rocky Mountains.
   - Ⓒ It is located in a desert in West Africa.
   - ● It is located on the North River in the Shenandoah Valley.

Lesson Objective (1:2)

4. What are some fun things to do in Bridgewater, Virginia?
   - Ⓐ go to the beach
   - ● go to Scouts and 4-H Club
   - Ⓒ visit museums
   - Ⓓ ski down mountains

Lesson Objective (1:4)

5. Which detail supports the following main idea? **If you like sports, Bridgewater is the place for you.**
   - Ⓐ The 4-H Club meets once a month to talk about farm issues.
   - Ⓑ Amy has lots of friends.
   - Ⓒ Bridgewater became the name of the town in 1835.
   - ● The Bridgewater All-Star baseball team has won the Virginia state championship.

Lesson Objective (2:1)

6. How is a suburban community different from a rural community?
   - Ⓐ Suburban communities have homes.
   - Ⓑ Suburban communities have stores.
   - ● Suburban communities are located near large cities.
   - Ⓓ Suburban communities have fun things to do.

Assessment Book Unit 1, Chapter 2 Test **5**

Chapter 2 Test

Lesson Objective (2:5)

7. Which main idea is supported by the following detail? **Levittown is just a train ride from New York City.**
   - Ⓐ Abraham Levitt began building homes in 1947.
   - ● Levittown, New York, is a suburb of New York City.
   - Ⓒ William Levitt helped his father plan and build their community.
   - Ⓓ New York City is the largest city in the United States.

Lesson Objective (2:4)

8. How are Levittown and Wilmington alike?
   - ● They both are located near the Atlantic Ocean.
   - Ⓑ They both are rural communities.
   - Ⓒ They both are located in North Carolina.
   - Ⓓ They both were started by Abraham Levitt.

Lesson Objective (2:3)

9. Why do people form communities?
   - ● They want to live and work where they feel safe and comfortable.
   - Ⓑ They like to grow potatoes.
   - Ⓒ They want to ride the train to the city.
   - Ⓓ They like to listen to concerts.

Lesson Objective (2:2)

10. How did Abraham Levitt and his family change a rural potato farm into a suburb?
    - ● They built many houses, schools, and parks.
    - Ⓑ They called their community Island Trees.
    - Ⓒ They rode the train to New York City.
    - Ⓓ They visited Jones Beach State Park.

Lesson Objective (3:1)

11. How is an urban community similar to a rural community?
    - ● Both have plenty of things to do.
    - Ⓑ Both have similar amounts of people.
    - Ⓒ Both have similar types of buildings.
    - Ⓓ Both have similar amounts of open land.

Lesson Objective (3:4)

12. Which detail supports the following main idea? **People in Chicago work in many places.**
    - Ⓐ The "El" is the elevated train that runs through Chicago.
    - Ⓑ In 1837 the town got the name *Chicago*.
    - ● Chicago has large department stores, banks, and office buildings.
    - Ⓓ Chicago is in the midwest part of the United States.

6 Unit 1, Chapter 2 Test Assessment Book

Chapter 2 Test

Lesson Objective (3:2)

13. How is Chicago different from Levittown?
    - Ⓐ There are homes, parks, and places of worship in Chicago.
    - Ⓑ People in Chicago drive cars to work.
    - Ⓒ Chicago is a great place to live.
    - ● Chicago is an important center of population and business activity.

Lesson Objective (3:2)

14. How are Chicago and Bridgewater alike?
    - ● There are fun things to do in both communities.
    - Ⓑ They are both suburban communities.
    - Ⓒ They are both large cities.
    - Ⓓ They both are located in the same state.

Lesson Objective (3:3)

15. What fun thing can you do in Chicago that you cannot do in Bridgewater?
    - Ⓐ attend 4-H meetings
    - ● visit the Art Institute
    - Ⓒ help others in your community
    - Ⓓ go to Scouts

Part 2: Skills Test

Directions: Use complete sentences to answer questions 1–5. Use a separate sheet of paper if you need more space.

1. Give three details to support the following main idea: **Bridgewater is a great place to live and go to school. Main Idea and Details**

   Possible answers: There are many things to do in Bridgewater (4-H Club, Scouting, and so on), the Little League baseball team won the Virginia state championship for the year 2000, everyone in town knows each other, helps each other out, and the children of the town play together.

Assessment Book Unit 1, Chapter 2 Test **7**

Chapter 2 Test

2. Write one fact and one opinion about Bridgewater, Virginia. Do you think that Amy likes living in her community? Why? **Fact and Opinion**

   Possible answer: Fact: Bridgewater is a rural community.

   Opinion: The Lawn Party is the best part of summer. Amy likes where she is; she names many exciting things to do.

3. Suppose your family is moving to a community where children enjoy going to 4-H Club meetings. What type of community might you be moving to? What will the towns be like there? What else might you and your friends do for fun? **Make Inferences**

   Possible answer: A rural community. The towns there will be small and far apart. Children can run and play in the open fields, be in Scouts, or play baseball.

4. Why is Lake Michigan important to Beth and her family? How do you know? **Draw Conclusions**

   Beth states that they enjoy watching boats sail there and going to the beach for picnics.

5. Suppose that one day the train system in Chicago stopped working. What might this mean for the people of that city? **Cause and Effect**

   If the trains did not work, many people would have to find another way to get around, buses and highways would become very crowded, and some people might have no way to get to work.

8 Unit 1, Chapter 2 Test Assessment Book

© Scott Foresman 3

---

74 Answer Key Assessment Book

Unit 1 Test

Part 1: Content Test

Directions: Fill in the circle next to the correct answer.

Lesson Objective (1–1:1)

1. What is a community?
   - Ⓐ It is a place that is on the border between two countries.
   - ● It is a place where people live, work, and have fun together.
   - Ⓒ It is a place where you can see into Mexico for miles.
   - Ⓓ It is a place that is more than 400 years old.

Lesson Objective (1–1:2)

2. How would you best describe the area where El Paso is located?
   - ● El Paso lies between two sets of mountains.
   - Ⓑ Many people live in El Paso.
   - Ⓒ El Paso is more than 400 years old.
   - Ⓓ El Paso was first settled by Native Americans.

Lesson Objective (1–1:3)

3. How is the history of El Paso different from that of many places in the United States?
   - Ⓐ In Juarez, Mexico, there are many places to eat and shop.
   - Ⓑ People work in and around the community of El Paso.
   - ● El Paso was first settled by Native Americans and then by Spaniards.
   - Ⓓ El Paso is on the border between Mexico and the United States.

Lesson Objective (1–2:1)

4. How is Astoria different from Wilmington?
   - Ⓐ Astoria is located on a river.
   - Ⓑ There are fun things to do in Astoria.
   - Ⓒ People live and work in Astoria.
   - ● Astoria is on the other side of the United States from Wilmington.

Lesson Objective (1–2:2)

5. In which state is Denver located?
   - ● Colorado
   - Ⓑ North Carolina
   - Ⓒ Texas
   - Ⓓ Oregon

Lesson Objective (1–2:4)

6. Which detail supports the following main idea? **Wilmington has some really cool places to visit.**
   - ● Visitors can go to Fort Fisher, a sand fort.
   - Ⓑ Wilmington is located in the state of North Carolina.
   - Ⓒ Anna's grandparents live in Wilmington.
   - Ⓓ A dot on the map shows where Wilmington is located.

Lesson Objective (1–2:3)

7. Where did the first settlers of Astoria move there from?
   - Ⓐ Spain
   - Ⓑ Arapaho
   - Ⓒ Texas
   - ● Scandinavia

Lesson Objective (1–3:1)

8. Which of the following is NOT a part of culture?
   - Ⓐ food
   - Ⓑ clothing
   - Ⓒ language
   - ● weather

Lesson Objective (1–3:2)

9. How has Timbuktu changed from earlier times?
   - Ⓐ Today Timbuktu is located on the continent of Africa.
   - ● Today many fewer people live in Timbuktu.
   - Ⓒ Today Timbuktu is located in a desert.
   - Ⓓ Today there are beautiful mosques in Timbuktu.

Lesson Objective (1–3:3)

10. What was Timbuktu like from the year 1400 to about 1600?
    - ● It was a very wealthy city.
    - Ⓑ It had only two great mosques.
    - Ⓒ Very few people lived there.
    - Ⓓ It was located in the United States of America.

Lesson Objective (2–1:1)

11. Where are rural communities located?
    - Ⓐ near large cities
    - Ⓑ by the water
    - Ⓒ in a desert
    - ● in the countryside

Lesson Objective (2–1:2)

12. What are some fun things to do in Bridgewater, Virginia?
    - Ⓐ ride the train into New York City and go to the beach
    - Ⓑ listen to concerts in Eisenhower Park
    - Ⓒ visit museums
    - ● go to Scouts and baseball games

Lesson Objective (2–2:4)

13. How are Bridgewater and Levittown alike?
    - Ⓐ Both communities have championship baseball teams.
    - Ⓑ People in both communities belong to the 4-H Club.
    - Ⓒ From both communities people can take a train to New York City.
    - ● Some people in both of these communities work in other communities.

Lesson Objective (2–2:3)

14. Why did Abraham Levitt build his community?
    - ● to make people living there feel safe and comfortable
    - Ⓑ so that people living there could go to Eisenhower Park
    - Ⓒ to locate it on Long Island
    - Ⓓ so that he could call it Island Trees

Lesson Objective (2–3:3)

15. What forms of transportation do many people in Chicago use?
    - Ⓐ They visit the Art Institute.
    - ● They use buses or the "El."
    - Ⓒ They ride horses or camels.
    - Ⓓ They watch boats sail on Lake Michigan.

Part 2: Skills Test

Directions: Use complete sentences to answer questions 1–3. Use a separate sheet of paper if you need more space.

1. Describe the area where your community is located. Why do you think it is located there? **Draw Conclusions**

   Possible answers should accurately reflect the area around the student's community and an understanding of how location affects a community.

2. How did Denver's location help it grow? **Cause and Effect**

   Possible answer: Many people want to visit and to live in the Rocky Mountains where Denver is located. Fur traders and prospectors also helped Denver grow.

---

3. How has Timbuktu changed between the year 1400 and today? **Compare and Contrast**

   From 1400 to about 1600, many thousands of people lived in Timbuktu. Today fewer people live there. Once there were three mosques in Timbuktu.

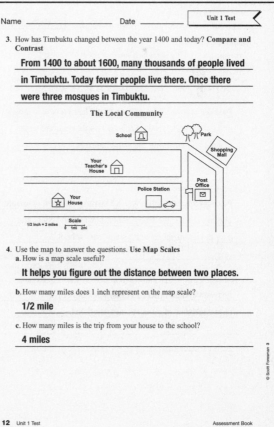

The Local Community

4. Use the map to answer the questions. **Use Map Scales**
   a. How is a map scale useful?

   It helps you figure out the distance between two places.

   b. How many miles does 1 inch represent on the map scale?

   1/2 mile

   c. How many miles is the trip from your house to the school?

   4 miles

Chapter 3 Test
Part 1: Content Test
Directions: Fill in the circle next to the correct answer.

Lesson Objective (1:1)

1. How is Tom similar to some students in his new class in Boston?
   - (A) Tom was born in Boston.
   - (B) Tom has always lived in Boston.
   - ● Tom moved to Boston from someplace else.
   - (D) Tom does not live in Boston.

Lesson Objective (1:1)

2. How is Tom different from some students in his new class in Boston?
   - ● Tom has not always lived in Boston.
   - (B) Tom has always lived in Boston.
   - (C) Tom has always lived outside the United States.
   - (D) Tom does not live in Boston.

Lesson Objective (1:1)

3. How is Tom's family similar to some families that move to the United States from other countries?
   - (A) Tom's family moved for freedom of religion.
   - (B) Tom's family moved for freedom of speech.
   - (C) Tom's family had to learn a new language.
   - ● Tom's family moved because of a job.

Lesson Objective (2:1, 3)

4. What can Nicole's new friends in Boston help her learn?
   - (A) soccer
   - ● English
   - (C) Haitian Creole
   - (D) Haitian customs

Lesson Objective (2:1, 4)

5. What is similar between Haiti and the United States?
   - ● school
   - (B) language
   - (C) customs
   - (D) neighborhoods

Lesson Objective (2:2)

6. What have Nicole and members of her ethnic group brought from Haiti to the United States?
   - (A) They brought their schools and buses.
   - (B) They left all of their customs behind in Haiti.
   - (C) They brought English and American foods.
   - ● They brought their language and other customs.

7. Which of the following is NOT a reason why immigrants formed communities in the United States?
   - (A) to feel safe
   - ● to escape new opportunities
   - (C) to set up good laws
   - (D) to make their lives better

Lesson Objective (3:2)

8. How can you tell that people in the United States come from different cultures and countries?
   - ● They speak many languages.
   - (B) They go to the same schools.
   - (C) They play soccer together.
   - (D) They eat similar foods.

Lesson Objective (3:5)

9. What are relatives that lived in past times called?
   - (A) immigrants
   - ● ancestors
   - (C) friends
   - (D) parents

Lesson Objective (3:5)

10. From which country did few people immigrate to the United States between 1861 and 1890?
   - (A) Germany
   - (B) Ireland
   - ● Mexico
   - (D) Sweden

Lesson Objective (4:1)

11. Why is it important for citizens of the United States to vote?
   - ● They can help make decisions that affect the community.
   - (B) They can live in apartments in ethnic neighborhoods.
   - (C) They can play games and sports brought to the United States by other groups.
   - (D) They can move from one part of the country to another in search of an opportunity.

Lesson Objective (4:4)

12. How is education today different from education in the past?
   - (A) Today children learn science.
   - (B) Today children learn mathematics.
   - (C) Today children begin school at a young age.
   - ● Today children learn about computers.

Lesson Objective (4:3)

13. What took place during the Great Migration?
   - (A) Many African Americans moved to the South.
   - ● Many African Americans moved to the North.
   - (C) Many African Americans moved to farms.
   - (D) Many African Americans moved to other countries.

Part 2: Skills Test
Directions: Use complete sentences to answer questions 1–5. Use a separate sheet of paper if you need more space.

1. Suppose that you and your family have lived in another country and are now moving to the United States. How do you think life will change? How might it remain the same? **Make Inferences**

   Possible answer: Different: we might learn a new language and eat different foods. Same: we might wear the same clothes and celebrate the same holidays.

2. How are your community and Nicole's ethnic neighborhood different? How are they alike? **Compare and Contrast**

   Possible answers: Different: we speak a different language at home. Same: we study similar subjects in school and play the same sports and games after school.

3. What are some positive reasons to live in an ethnic neighborhood? Do you think there are any negative reasons? If so, what are they? **Express Ideas**

   Answers should reflect an understanding of the characteristics of an ethnic neighborhood.

4. Why do you think the Statue of Liberty is a symbol of freedom for many people? **Interpret National Symbols**

   Possible answer: The Statue of Liberty is a symbol of freedom for many immigrants because it is the first thing they saw when they arrived in this country. It meant their trip was over, and they could begin a new life.

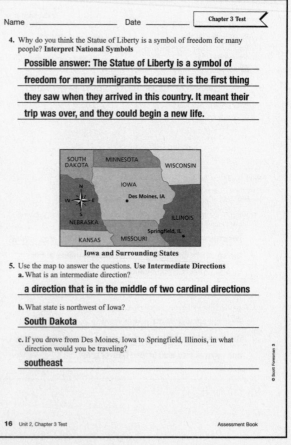

Iowa and Surrounding States

5. Use the map to answer the questions. **Use Intermediate Directions**
   a. What is an intermediate direction?

   a direction that is in the middle of two cardinal directions

   b. What state is northwest of Iowa?

   South Dakota

   c. If you drove from Des Moines, Iowa to Springfield, Illinois, in what direction would you be traveling?

   southeast

Chapter 4 Test

Part 1: Content Test

Directions: Fill in the circle next to the correct answer.

Lesson Objective (1:1)

1. Which holiday celebrates the end of Ramadan?
   - ● Eid-al-Fitr
   - Ⓑ Christmas
   - Ⓒ Hanukkah
   - Ⓓ Kwanzaa

Lesson Objective (1:1)

2. Why do many families celebrate Kwanzaa?
   - Ⓐ They like to light candles and sing songs.
   - Ⓑ They enjoy giving gifts to family members.
   - ● They want to honor their ancestors.
   - Ⓓ They are hungry for a large meal with special sweets.

Lesson Objective (1:2)

3. How is Christmas different from Kwanzaa?
   - Ⓐ Families light red, green, and black candles for Christmas.
   - Ⓑ Christmas honors African American culture.
   - Ⓒ Christmas lasts for seven days.
   - ● Families decorate trees and celebrate the birth of Jesus on Christmas.

Lesson Objective (1:2)

4. How are Christmas, Hanukkah, and Eid-al-Fitr alike?
   - Ⓐ Families light eight candles during all three holidays.
   - Ⓑ Families celebrate for seven days during all three holidays.
   - ● Families share a special meal or eat special foods at all three holidays.
   - Ⓓ Families decorate trees for all three holidays.

Lesson Objective (1:1)

5. What do people celebrate on St. Patrick's Day?
   - Ⓐ a corn harvest
   - Ⓑ green clothing
   - Ⓒ life in Europe
   - ● Irish culture

Lesson Objective (1:2)

6. How are Cinco de Mayo and St. Patrick's Day alike?
   - Ⓐ People eat green-dyed food to celebrate both.
   - ● They both show that people are proud of their culture.
   - Ⓒ They are both celebrated on the fifth of May.
   - Ⓓ They both started in the country of Ireland.

Lesson Objective (2:1)

7. What makes the heritage festival in New Orleans unique?
   - ● It honors the history and culture of the people of New Orleans.
   - Ⓑ It honors the person who started New Orleans.
   - Ⓒ It honors the work people in Louisiana have done that year.
   - Ⓓ It celebrates the harvest.

Lesson Objective (2:1)

8. Why do many communities hold their own special celebrations?
   - Ⓐ to show livestock to the community members
   - Ⓑ to pass out ribbons to winners of contests
   - Ⓒ to celebrate the corn harvest
   - ● to bring the people of the community together

Lesson Objective (2:1)

9. What special event is held each year in Hutchinson, Kansas?
   - ● state fair
   - Ⓑ heritage festival
   - Ⓒ jazz festival
   - Ⓓ world's fair

Lesson Objective (3:2)

10. On what day do we honor people who fought and died for the United States?
    - Ⓐ the fifth of May
    - Ⓑ the third Monday in January
    - Ⓒ the third Thursday in November
    - ● the last Monday in May

Lesson Objective (3:2)

11. What two holidays honor people who fought for the United States?
    - Ⓐ Memorial Day and Thanksgiving Day
    - ● Veterans Day and Memorial Day
    - Ⓒ Cinco de Mayo and Veterans Day
    - Ⓓ Memorial Day and St. Patrick's Day

Lesson Objective (3:1)

12. What did Dr. King fight for?
    - Ⓐ He fought for a holiday held the third Monday in January.
    - ● He fought for all people to be treated equally.
    - Ⓒ He fought for freedom for the United States.
    - Ⓓ He fought for the freedom to choose the government.

Lesson Objective (3:1)

13. What was the name of the drive that Dr. Martin Luther King, Jr., led?
    - Ⓐ African Americans
    - Ⓑ Thanksgiving
    - ● Civil Rights Movement
    - Ⓓ Memorial Day

Lesson Objective (3:1)

14. What did Dr. King use to convince people to make changes?
    - Ⓐ computers
    - Ⓑ fists
    - Ⓒ bombs
    - ● words

Part 2: Skills Test

Directions: Use complete sentences to answer questions 1–4. Use a separate sheet of paper if you need more space.

1. Why do you think many families celebrate holidays by sharing a special meal? **Draw Conclusions**

   Possible answer: Families have a special meal to enjoy time together talking around the table and to share special dishes they have prepared with love for their family members.

2. Cinco de Mayo, Memorial Day, and Veterans Day all honor people who have fought in battles. Why do you think communities find it important to remember them? **Make Inferences**

   Possible answer: People want to honor those who fought for freedom, independence, and other important issues.

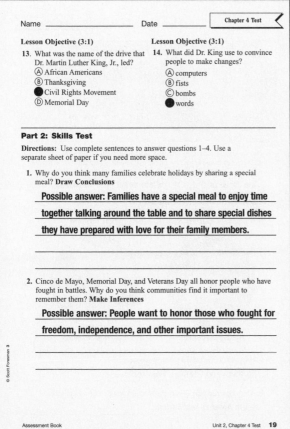

3. The United States has a national holiday to honor Dr. Martin Luther King, Jr. Think of another person, either living or dead, whom you believe should have his or her own holiday. Why should that person have a day in his or her honor? **Express Ideas**

   Possible answer: The current President should have a holiday to honor his birthday. The President works hard for our country.

4. What is your favorite holiday? Compare and contrast it with one of the holidays from your textbook. **Compare and Contrast**

   Possible answer: My favorite holiday is Labor Day. Like Memorial Day, it is a national holiday, but I don't watch a parade on Labor Day.

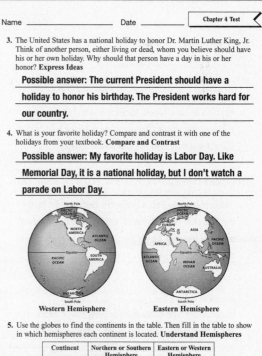

Western Hemisphere   **Eastern Hemisphere**

5. Use the globes to find the continents in the table. Then fill in the table to show in which hemispheres each continent is located. **Understand Hemispheres**

Continent	Northern or Southern Hemisphere	Eastern or Western Hemisphere
North America	Northern	Western
Asia	Northern	Eastern
South America	Both	Western
Europe	Northern	Western

© Scott Foresman 3

Unit 2 Test

Part 1: Content Test

Directions: Fill in the circle next to the correct answer.

Lesson Objective (3–1:1)

1. What do many people who move to a new city have in common with many who move to a new country?
   - ● Both want to find a better life.
   - Ⓑ Both want to become U.S. citizens.
   - Ⓒ Both want to find religious freedom.
   - Ⓓ Both want to stay in their neighborhood.

Lesson Objective (3–2:1)

2. Why do people set up systems of laws in their communities?
   - ● to make the community safe
   - Ⓑ to make new friends in their community
   - Ⓒ to go to a new school in the community
   - Ⓓ to find a better job in the community

Lesson Objective (3–3:2)

3. Which of the following does NOT show that the United States is home to many cultures?
   - Ⓐ different languages
   - Ⓑ different clothing
   - Ⓒ different foods
   - ● different communities

Lesson Objective (3–2:1, 3)

4. How do ethnic neighborhoods help people who move to this country?
   - Ⓐ People can learn English very quickly since that is the only language spoken in an ethnic neighborhood.
   - Ⓑ People can buy American foods in an ethnic neighborhood in the United States.
   - ● People can get used to a new culture while still being around their old culture.
   - Ⓓ People can ride buses and talk to friends from their home country on the phone.

Lesson Objective (3–3:5)

5. What is the word for "relatives who lived in past times"?
   - Ⓐ decades
   - Ⓑ symbols
   - ● ancestors
   - Ⓓ immigrants

Lesson Objective (3–3:1)

6. For what reason have Tom's family and many other families moved to a new city?
   - ● for a better job
   - Ⓑ to get a health test
   - Ⓒ to see Ellis Island
   - Ⓓ to become famous writers

Lesson Objective (3–3:4)

7. What is a benefit of becoming a citizen of the United States?
   - ● A citizen can vote to help make decisions.
   - Ⓑ A citizen can visit the museum at Ellis Island.
   - Ⓒ A citizen can learn a new language.
   - Ⓓ A citizen can migrate from one part of the country to another.

Lesson Objective (3–3:3)

8. What made Langston Hughes famous?
   - Ⓐ dancing
   - ● writing
   - Ⓒ singing
   - Ⓓ painting

Lesson Objective (4–1:1)

9. What is celebrated on St. Patrick's Day?
   - Ⓐ Jewish ancestors
   - Ⓑ Christian families
   - ● Irish culture
   - Ⓓ jazz music

Lesson Objective (4–2:1)

10. What is special about Hutchinson, Kansas?
    - Ⓐ Pilgrims settled there.
    - Ⓑ The New Orleans Jazz and Heritage Festival is held there.
    - ● The Kansas State Fair is held there.
    - Ⓓ The Tomb of the Unknown Soldier is located there.

Lesson Objective (4–2:2)

11. How is the Kansas State Fair like the New Orleans Jazz and Heritage Festival?
    - Ⓐ They both honor the history of the people of New Orleans.
    - ● They both bring the people of the community together.
    - Ⓒ They both celebrate the hard work of the people of Kansas.
    - Ⓓ They both are held in September, when the crops are ready to eat.

Lesson Objective (4–3:2)

12. Who do Americans honor on Memorial Day and Veterans Day?
    - ● the people who fought for the United States
    - Ⓑ the leaders of the Civil Rights Movement
    - Ⓒ the Wampanoag Indians
    - Ⓓ the settlers of Plymouth

Lesson Objective (4–3:1)

13. Why do Americans celebrate the life of Dr. Martin Luther King, Jr.?
    - Ⓐ He painted a famous picture of George Washington.
    - Ⓑ He fought for freedom for the United States.
    - ● He fought for all people to be treated equally.
    - Ⓓ He helped the Pilgrims grow their crops.

Part 2: Skills Test

Directions: Use complete sentences to answer questions 1–3. Use a separate sheet of paper if you need more space.

1. Tom and Nicole both just moved to Boston. Which one might find the move more difficult? Why? How might they help each other with their new life in Boston? **Hypothesize**

   Possible answer: Nicole, because she had to learn new customs and a new language; they could be friends and learn about their new city and school together.

2. How were the immigrants of the early 1900s similar to and different from the African Americans of the Great Migration? **Compare and Contrast**

   Same: both moved for a better life. Both brought their cultures with them. Different: African Americans moved from the southern part of the United States. They already spoke English.

3. Why do communities hold special celebrations? What effect do these festivals and fairs have on life in the community? **Cause and Effect**

   Communities hold celebrations to bring people together. These celebrations show the people of the community that they are special. Celebrations are a fun way for people to get together and meet each other.

4. Use the map to answer the questions. **Use Intermediate Directions**
   a. What does the compass rose on the bottom left corner tell you? What are the four intermediate directions?

   the cardinal and intermediate directions; northeast, southeast, southwest, northwest

   b. What state is southwest of Pennsylvania? **West Virginia**

   Western Hemisphere   **Eastern Hemisphere**

5. Study the globes and then answer the questions. **Understand Hemispheres**
   a. What two hemispheres does the equator separate?

   Northern and Southern Hemispheres

   b. Which continents are in both the Northern and Southern Hemispheres?

   South America and Africa

     Assessment Book

Chapter 5 Test
Part 1: Content Test
Directions: Fill in the circle next to the correct answer.

Lesson Objective (1:1)

1. Which community is in the Western region of the United States?
   - Ⓐ Stamford, Connecticut
   - Ⓑ Charleston, South Carolina
   - ● Bozeman, Montana
   - Ⓓ Omaha, Nebraska

Lesson Objective (1:2)

2. Which of these is a landform that you can see in the Southwest region of the United States?
   - Ⓐ cactuses
   - Ⓑ snakes
   - ● canyons
   - Ⓓ bridges

Lesson Objective (1:4)

3. Farmers in the Southwest region bring in water for their crops. How has this changed their region?
   - ● Many plants that could not grow there now grow very well.
   - Ⓑ Many plants have died from too much water.
   - Ⓒ Many trees have been cut to clear land for planting crops.
   - Ⓓ Many plants cannot live there because of the cold weather.

Lesson Objective (1:2)

4. How is the physical environment in Omaha, Nebraska, different from that in Bozeman, Montana?
   - ● Omaha has no mountains.
   - Ⓑ A river runs through Omaha.
   - Ⓒ The weather in Omaha is cold all year long.
   - Ⓓ Omaha has many mountains.

Lesson Objective (1:3)

5. What have people done to forests to meet human needs?
   - Ⓐ They bring in water so the trees can grow.
   - Ⓑ They heat their homes and offices.
   - Ⓒ They wear warm clothing, such as hats and scarves.
   - ● They cut the trees to use for lumber to build houses.

Lesson Objective (2:1)

6. Why is the climate in Kauai, Hawaii, different from the climate in Barrow, Alaska?
   - Ⓐ Kauai is much higher than Barrow.
   - Ⓑ Kauai is much farther away from the equator than Barrow.
   - Ⓒ Barrow is in the Northeast region.
   - ● Kauai is much closer to the equator than Barrow.

Lesson Objective (2:3)

7. Which should you NOT take to wear on a vacation in Kauai?
   - Ⓐ a bathing suit
   - ● a winter coat
   - Ⓒ sunglasses
   - Ⓓ shorts and T-shirts

Lesson Objective (2:3)

8. Which activity might people living in Barrow NOT enjoy doing there?
   - Ⓐ ice skating
   - Ⓑ snow skiing
   - ● swimming outdoors
   - Ⓓ snow mobiling

Lesson Objective (2:2)

9. How have the Pueblo adapted to the climate in Taos?
   - Ⓐ They wear warm coats all year long.
   - Ⓑ They make beautiful pottery to sell in the markets.
   - Ⓒ They live on the plateau surrounded by mountains.
   - ● They have built adobe houses with thick walls.

Lesson Objective (3:3)

10. Which was an important natural resource in California?
   - Ⓐ oil
   - Ⓑ miners
   - Ⓒ homes
   - ● gold

Lesson Objective (3:1)

11. How were the settlers at Angel's Camp different from the people of Beaumont, Texas?
   - ● At Angel's Camp, they dug deep into the earth looking for gold.
   - Ⓑ At Angel's Camp, they drilled wells looking for pockets of oil.
   - Ⓒ The settlers moved to Angel's Camp to work in the oil fields.
   - Ⓓ The settlers called what they had found "black gold."

Lesson Objective (3:2)

12. What are two ways to conserve natural resources?
   - Ⓐ use as much of them as you can and recycle them
   - Ⓑ dig deep into the earth and use less of them
   - Ⓒ recycle them and dig oil wells
   - ● use less of them and recycle them

Lesson Objective (3:3)

13. What would happen if we used up all the fuels on Earth?
   - ● We would have to find new sources of energy.
   - Ⓑ We would stay warm in our heated homes.
   - Ⓒ We would have all the light we needed.
   - Ⓓ We would have to look for more gold and salt.

Part 2: Skills Test
Directions: Use complete sentences to answer questions 1–4. Use a separate sheet of paper if you need more space.

1. Suppose that you live in a region with many forests, hills, and mountains. What problems might you face in trying to build roads and railways there? How can you solve those problems? **Solve Problems**

   It would be difficult to build a road or railway through a dense forest or over hills and mountains. I would have to cut down trees in the forest to make paths. I would have to go around hills or make them smaller. I would have to go around or cut through mountains to make roads and tracks.

2. What is the physical environment of your community like? Describe its landforms and climate, as well as the plants, animals, and resources that can be found there. **Apply Information**

   Answers should reflect an understanding of the physical environment of the students' community.

3. Which region of the United States would you most like to live in? Why? **Express Ideas**

   Answers should express an understanding of the selected region.

---

4. What type of people moved to California in search of gold? Describe someone who would follow the Gold Rush. **Draw Conclusions**

   Possible answer: Those people would have to like adventure and be brave. They would have to not mind moving from their homes and friends to a new community.

5. Use the graph to answer the questions. **Use a Line Graph**
   a. What does the graph show?

   the average high temperatures for four months in Louisville, Kentucky

   b. What do the numbers on the side of the graph tell you?

   the temperature in degrees Fahrenheit

   c. Which month has the warmest high temperature? What is that temperature?

   June; 83 degrees Fahrenheit

   Average High Temperature in Louisville, Kentucky

   (Line graph: Temperature (°F) vs Month — January 39, February 44, March 55, April 66, May 74, June 83)

© Scott Foresman 3

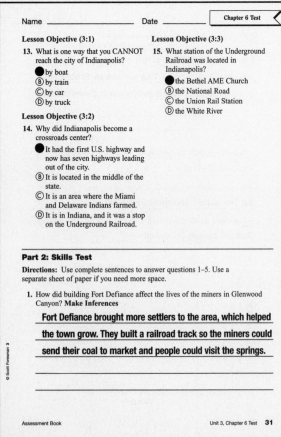

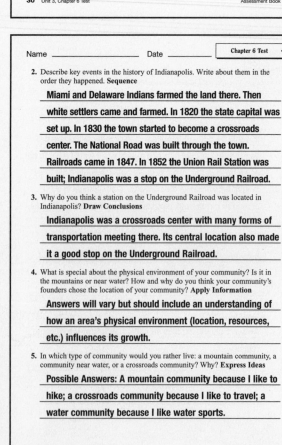

Chapter 6 Test

Part 1: Content Test

Directions: Fill in the circle next to the correct answer.

Lesson Objective (1:1)

1. Who set up Fort Defiance and then later named it Glenwood Springs?
   A Glenwood Canyon
   B the Ute Indians
   ● Captain Isaac Cooper
   D Colorado Midland Railroad

Lesson Objective (1:1)

2. How did the railroad help the community of Glenwood Springs?
   ● Miners had a way to send their coal to other communities.
   B Miners were able to dig for materials from the earth.
   C The land was able to be settled by the Ute Indians.
   D The community changed its name to Fort Defiance.

Lesson Objective (1:2)

3. Why was it hard for railroad workers to build tracks into Glenwood Springs?
   A They had to build around the hot water springs.
   B They had to build through the desert.
   C They had to cut down trees to build through the forest.
   ● They had to build through the mountains.

Lesson Objective (1:5)

4. Which type of person would be most able to start a mountain community?
   A an impatient person
   ● a patient person
   C a tired person
   D a lazy person

Lesson Objective (2:1)

5. What happened in 1851 to make the city of Seattle start to grow?
   A One of the Native American leaders was Chief Sealth.
   B Puget Sound is located near the Pacific Ocean.
   C The area around Seattle has many trees.
   ● A group of settlers built a town on Alki Point.

Lesson Objective (2:2)

6. Which of these is NOT an important natural resource in Seattle?
   A water
   ● gold
   C trees
   D fish

Assessment Book   Unit 3, Chapter 6 Test   29

Lesson Objective (2:1)

7. Why did the settlers name their town in honor of Chief Sealth?
   ● He was friendly to them and helped them.
   B He built all of their houses for them.
   C He showed them how to cook fish.
   D He moved to Puget Sound to be near them.

Lesson Objective (2:3)

8. What became an important industry around Seattle because of a natural resource there?
   A fishing
   B computer building
   ● logging
   D airplane making

Lesson Objective (2:3)

9. How did the water around Seattle help it grow?
   ● Its port is a place where ships come and go from around the world.
   B Airplane making and computer companies need water to build their products.
   C People who enjoy water sports moved to Seattle to be near the ocean.
   D Loggers can make money and build their businesses by sailing on the ocean.

Lesson Objective (2:4)

10. What might happen to the water around Seattle if the city continues to grow?
    A The people who live in Seattle might someday use all the natural resources, including the water.
    B Computer companies will become larger.
    ● The ships that come to the port and the people who live in Seattle might pollute the water.
    D The loggers might use up all of the water by cutting down trees and making lumber.

Lesson Objective (3:4)

11. What happened to Indianapolis in 1820 that is still true today?
    A It became a crossroads center.
    B The Miami Indians farmed there.
    C The National Road was built.
    ● It became the state capital.

Lesson Objective (3:2)

12. How did the National Road help the people of the United States?
    A People from the North moved south using the road.
    ● People from the East moved west using the road.
    C People from the West moved east using the road.
    D People could travel around Indianapolis more easily.

30   Unit 3, Chapter 6 Test   Assessment Book

Lesson Objective (3:1)

13. What is one way that you CANNOT reach the city of Indianapolis?
    ● by boat
    B by train
    C by car
    D by truck

Lesson Objective (3:2)

14. Why did Indianapolis become a crossroads center?
    ● It had the first U.S. highway and now has seven highways leading out of the city.
    B It is located in the middle of the state.
    C It is an area where the Miami and Delaware Indians farmed.
    D It is in Indiana, and it was a stop on the Underground Railroad.

Lesson Objective (3:3)

15. What station of the Underground Railroad was located in Indianapolis?
    ● the Bethel AME Church
    B the National Road
    C the Union Rail Station
    D the White River

Part 2: Skills Test

Directions: Use complete sentences to answer questions 1–5. Use a separate sheet of paper if you need more space.

1. How did building Fort Defiance affect the lives of the miners in Glenwood Canyon? Make Inferences

   Fort Defiance brought more settlers to the area, which helped the town grow. They built a railroad track so the miners could send their coal to market and people could visit the springs.

Assessment Book   Unit 3, Chapter 6 Test   31

2. Describe key events in the history of Indianapolis. Write about them in the order they happened. Sequence

   Miami and Delaware Indians farmed the land there. Then white settlers came and farmed. In 1820 the state capital was set up. In 1830 the town started to become a crossroads center. The National Road was built through the town. Railroads came in 1847. In 1852 the Union Rail Station was built; Indianapolis was a stop on the Underground Railroad.

3. Why do you think a station on the Underground Railroad was located in Indianapolis? Draw Conclusions

   Indianapolis was a crossroads center with many forms of transportation meeting there. Its central location also made it a good stop on the Underground Railroad.

4. What is special about the physical environment of your community? Is it in the mountains or near water? How and why do you think your community's founders chose the location of your community? Apply Information

   Answers will vary but should include an understanding of how an area's physical environment (location, resources, etc.) influences its growth.

5. In which type of community would you rather live: a mountain community, a community near water, or a crossroads community? Why? Express Ideas

   Possible Answers: A mountain community because I like to hike; a crossroads community because I like to travel; a water community because I like water sports.

32   Unit 3, Chapter 6 Test   Assessment Book

© Scott Foresman 3

Unit 3 Test

Part 1: Content Test

Directions: Fill in the circle next to the correct answer.

Lesson Objective (5–1:1)

1. Which of these is a community in the Midwest region of the United States?
● Omaha, Nebraska
Ⓑ Bozeman, Montana
Ⓒ Kauai, Hawaii
Ⓓ Tucson, Arizona

Lesson Objective (5–1:2; 5–2:1)

2. How are the landforms in Bozeman different from those in Omaha?
Ⓐ The land around Bozeman is flat.
Ⓑ Bozeman is surrounded by a desert.
Ⓒ A river runs through the town of Bozeman.
● Bozeman is surrounded by mountains.

Lesson Objective (5–2:2)

3. What fun activity are people NOT able to enjoy in Omaha, Nebraska?
Ⓐ walking along paths
● boating on the ocean
Ⓒ biking in the town
Ⓓ playing in the park

Lesson Objective (5–1:5)

4. Which landform makes it possible for people in the Western region to enjoy snow skiing?
Ⓐ plateau
Ⓑ desert
● mountain
Ⓓ canyon

Lesson Objective (5–1:3, 4; 5–2:2; 6–1:2)

5. What important change to the environment do the farmers of the Southwest region make?
Ⓐ They cut down trees to build their houses.
Ⓑ They build railroads through the canyons.
● They bring in water to help grow their crops.
Ⓓ They dig for minerals to feed their crops.

Lesson Objective (5–3:2)

6. What is one way to conserve natural resources?
Ⓐ by using as much of them as you can
● by using less of them
Ⓒ by using more of them
Ⓓ by using them only once

Lesson Objective (5–3:3)

7. Why is it important to conserve fuels?
Ⓐ Conserving fuels helps scientists find new sources of energy.
Ⓑ Once fuel is recycled, it can never be used again.
Ⓒ There are so many fuels that it is not possible to use them up.
● Fuels are natural resources that can become used up.

Lesson Objective (6–1:3)

8. What did Captain Isaac Cooper do to help the area of Glenwood Canyon?
● He set up Fort Defiance.
Ⓑ He dug deep into the earth.
Ⓒ He built railroad tracks.
Ⓓ He discovered hot springs there.

Lesson Objective (6–1:1)

9. Why was the discovery of hot springs in Glenwood Canyon important?
Ⓐ The Ute Indians were able to settle in the area of Glenwood Canyon.
Ⓑ The miners were finally able to send their coal out to other communities.
Ⓒ The Colorado Midland Railroad was able to build tracks through the mountains.
● Many people came to visit the springs, settled there, and the town of Glenwood Springs grew.

Lesson Objective (6–2:3)

10. How did logging become an important industry in Seattle?
Ⓐ Airplanes are made in Seattle.
● Seattle has many trees.
Ⓒ Chief Sealth helped the settlers.
Ⓓ Fish are an important resource.

Lesson Objective (6–2:4)

11. What should loggers do to make sure that their industry continues to grow around Seattle?
● plant trees to take the place of the ones they cut
Ⓑ continue to use the port in Seattle to ship wood
Ⓒ help the computer companies grow
Ⓓ buy airplanes that are built in Seattle

Lesson Objective (6–3:2)

12. What happened in Indianapolis in the 1830s?
Ⓐ Union Rail Station was built there.
● The National Road was built there.
Ⓒ Several highways passed through there.
Ⓓ Many people farmed there.

Lesson Objective (6–3:1)

13. What is one way that the businesses of Indianapolis can send their products to the rest of the country?
● by truck on the highways leading out of the city
Ⓑ by ship on the river that runs through the city
Ⓒ by barge on the lake that is near the city
Ⓓ by ship on the ocean by which the city is located

Lesson Objective (6–3:3)

14. Who used the Underground Railroad in Indianapolis?
Ⓐ loggers sending wood to the nearest port
Ⓑ government workers using the National Road
● African American slaves escaping from the South to the North
Ⓓ People working in the airplane and computer industries

Part 1: Skills Test

Directions: Use complete sentences to answer questions 1–5. Use a separate sheet of paper if you need more space.

1. Suppose that Katrinka and her family move from Bozeman, Montana, to Tucson, Arizona. What will she have to do to adapt to her new environment? What activities will she have to leave behind in Bozeman? **Hypothesize**

   Katrinka will need to wear cooler clothes to adapt to a warmer climate. She can still paddle her kayak and go hiking. She probably cannot ski there.

2. How does each region's environment affect the animals that live there? Why do alligators live in the Southeast? **Make Inferences**

   The plants and animals of a region have to adapt to its landforms and climate.

---

3. Why do you think new industries are choosing to start in Seattle? **Draw Conclusions**

   Seattle has many natural resources. The port in Seattle is a place where ships load and unload goods from around the world. A new industry would have a way to get its products shipped to many places if it were located in Seattle.

4. Do you think Indianapolis will continue to be an important city in the United States? Why or why not? What might happen in its future? **Predict**

   Indianapolis might continue to grow because of its location and the railroads and highways that go through it.

Average Monthly Snowfall in Helena, MT

5. Use the graph to answer the questions. **Use a Line Graph**
   a. Why is reading the title of this graph important?

   The title tells what the graph shows.

   b. What do the numbers along the side of the graph tell?

   the amount of snowfall in inches

   c. How much snow falls in Helena in May?

   about 1 1/2 inches

Chapter 7 Test

Part 1: Content Test

Directions: Fill in the circle next to the correct answer.

Lesson Objective (1:2)

1. Europeans explored both New York and Quebec, Canada. How were those two areas similar?
   - ● Native Americans already lived in both places.
   - B Both places were full of beautiful flowers.
   - C Explorers found golden cities in both places.
   - D The Iroquois farmed in both places.

Lesson Objective (1:1, 4)

2. How did the early Iroquois women use the land where they lived?
   - A They gathered wild berries.
   - B They dug pits to cook food.
   - ● They grew crops, such as corn.
   - D They planted flowers.

Lesson Objective (1:2)

3. What is one accomplishment shared by Columbus, De Soto, and Ponce de León?
   - ● They all explored North America for Spain.
   - B They all sailed from Portugal to South America.
   - C They all landed in present-day Canada.
   - D They all competed against French explorers.

Lesson Objective (1:2)

4. Which of these explorers landed in Canada?
   - A Hernando de Soto
   - B Juan Ponce de León
   - C Christopher Columbus
   - ● Jacques Cartier

Lesson Objective (2:1, 2)

5. Who first gave the state of Florida its name?
   - ● Juan Ponce de León
   - B Samuel de Champlain
   - C Christopher Columbus
   - D King Philip II of Spain

Lesson Objective (2:1, 2)

6. After Ponce de León left Florida, what country continued to explore there?
   - ● Spain
   - B Canada
   - C North America
   - D South America

Lesson Objective (2:3)

7. Who led the group that built the first permanent European settlement of St. Augustine?
   - A Christopher Columbus
   - B Jacques Cartier
   - ● Don Pedro Menéndez de Avilés
   - D Samuel de Champlain

Lesson Objective (3:2)

8. What European group explored both Florida and Canada?
   - ● French
   - B Spanish
   - C Portuguese
   - D Dutch

Lesson Objective (3:1)

9. Why did Jacques Cartier leave Canada to go back to France?
   - A Menéndez and his men drove Cartier away.
   - ● Rapids and falls blocked his westward path to China.
   - C Champlain told him to return to France.
   - D He was defeated at Quebec City by the English.

Lesson Objective (3:2)

10. Which present-day city is in the same place that Champlain built a settlement?
   - A St. Augustine, Florida
   - ● Quebec City, Quebec
   - C Champaign, Illinois
   - D Oneida County, New York

Lesson Objective (3:3)

11. How was Champlain different from Cartier?
   - A Champlain was French.
   - B Champlain explored Canada.
   - ● Champlain built a settlement.
   - D Champlain found a route to China.

Lesson Objective (4:1)

12. Who took 105 men on a ship from England to settle in North America?
   - A Chief Powhatan
   - B John Smith
   - ● Christopher Newport
   - D Christopher Columbus

Lesson Objective (4:1)

13. In which state is Jamestown located?
   - ● Virginia
   - B Quebec
   - C Florida
   - D New York

Lesson Objective (4:2)

14. How are the settlements of St. Augustine and Jamestown alike?
   - A They are both located in the state of Florida.
   - ● They are both still towns in the United States.
   - C They were both founded by the English.
   - D They were both captured by Native Americans.

Lesson Objective (4:3)

15. Why did the first English settlers come to North America?
   - A to elect representatives
   - B to choose their government
   - C to plant crops
   - ● to seek their fortune

Part 2: Skills Test

Directions: Use complete sentences to answer questions 1–5. Use a separate sheet of paper if you need more space.

1. How might an Iroquois living in Oneida County feel about the arrival of the European explorers? What conflicts do you think developed? **Draw Conclusions**

   Possible answers: An Iroquois might have felt invaded since explorers came seeking land already occupied by them. Conflicts over territory probably happened.

2. What effects do you think Ponce de León had on the Native Americans living in Florida? **Cause and Effect**

   Possible answer: Native Americans faced losing their religion, language, culture, and land.

3. How is Quebec City today like it was when it was first built? How is it different? What events in the city's history helped to change it? **Compare and Contrast**

   Today Quebec City is still located in the same place as it was when it was first settled. Much of the city has grown and changed. The defeat of the French by the English helped change Quebec City to what it is today.

4. Why is the history of Jamestown, Virginia, important to us today? **Draw Conclusions**

   The meeting of the first representative assembly in North America took place in Jamestown. This is important today because it started a foundation for what the United States government would become.

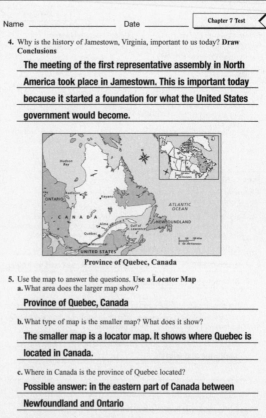

Province of Quebec, Canada

5. Use the map to answer the questions. **Use a Locator Map**
   a. What area does the larger map show?

   Province of Quebec, Canada

   b. What type of map is the smaller map? What does it show?

   The smaller map is a locator map. It shows where Quebec is located in Canada.

   c. Where in Canada is the province of Quebec located?

   Possible answer: in the eastern part of Canada between Newfoundland and Ontario

Chapter 8 Test

Part 1: Content Test

Directions: Fill in the circle next to the correct answer.

Lesson Objective (1:1)

1. What is one reason that new communities grew in the West?
   - ● Lewis and Clark told interesting stories about the West.
   - Ⓑ The trip along the Oregon Trail took six months.
   - Ⓒ People liked riding together in wagon trains.
   - Ⓓ The journey to the West was difficult and dangerous.

Lesson Objective (1:3)

2. How did James Watt and Richard Trevithick help families moving west?
   - Ⓐ They opened the Transcontinental Railroad.
   - Ⓑ They guided Lewis and Clark to the Pacific Ocean.
   - Ⓒ They led wagon trains down the Oregon Trail.
   - ● They developed and improved steam engines.

Lesson Objective (2:3)

3. Which inventor used a special tube to build a television?
   - Ⓐ Orville Wright
   - Ⓑ Benjamin Franklin
   - ● A. A. Campbell Swinton
   - Ⓓ Gottlieb Daimler

Lesson Objective (1:2)

4. How was travel in the United States in 1917 different from travel in 1830?
   - Ⓐ In 1917 Daimler and Benz invented the first gasoline-powered car.
   - ● In 1917 there were over 250,000 more miles of railroad track than in 1830.
   - Ⓒ In 1917 most people traveled across the United States on horseback.
   - Ⓓ In 1917 many people flew on airplanes to places all over the world.

Lesson Objective (2:4)

5. Which is NOT a reason why the Pony Express was set up?
   - Ⓐ People in the West wanted to communicate with the East.
   - Ⓑ Bandits often attacked wagons loaded with mail.
   - ● Many people liked to ride their horses 75 miles per day.
   - Ⓓ Weather often caused delays for the wagon trains.

Lesson Objective (2:1)

6. Why was mail delivered more quickly starting in 1860 than it had been before?
   - ● A group of business people set up the Pony Express.
   - Ⓑ People were able to send their letters by email.
   - Ⓒ Letters were sent on the Transcontinental Railroad.
   - Ⓓ In 1860 Samuel Morse invented the telegraph.

Lesson Objective (3:1)

7. Which is NOT an accomplishment of Lewis Latimer?
   - Ⓐ He did special drawings of a telephone.
   - ● He invented a way to develop a picture.
   - Ⓒ He worked on lamps and light bulbs with Edison.
   - Ⓓ He helped many cities light their communities.

Lesson Objective (3:2)

8. What did George Eastman invent in 1888?
   - ● He invented a camera that anyone could use to take a picture.
   - Ⓑ He invented a type of picture that appeared on a piece of metal.
   - Ⓒ He invented a sharp blade with a long handle for harvesting crops.
   - Ⓓ He invented a way to light factories and homes.

Lesson Objective (4:2)

9. Why is Louis Pasteur an important scientist to people around the world?
   - ● He made milk safe for people to drink.
   - Ⓑ He invented a way to light people's homes.
   - Ⓒ He helped people fight off smallpox.
   - Ⓓ He created many types of machines.

Lesson Objective (4:3)

10. Why is Jonas Salk's polio vaccine important?
    - Ⓐ The vaccine harms a person's healthy cells.
    - Ⓑ The vaccine destroys a person's spinal cord.
    - Ⓒ The vaccine did not work.
    - ● The vaccine saved the lives of many people.

Lesson Objective (4:1, 3)

11. Which is NOT an accomplishment of Gertrude Elion?
    - Ⓐ She helped treat people who had leukemia and malaria.
    - ● She developed a way to kill off certain germs in milk.
    - Ⓒ She figured out how to make medicine to attack diseased cells.
    - Ⓓ She won a Nobel Prize for her work in medicine.

Lesson Objective (3:3)

12. What did Cyrus Hall McCormick invent to make farming easier?
    - Ⓐ horse
    - Ⓑ lamp
    - Ⓒ camera
    - ● reaper

Lesson Objective (4:1)

13. Who found a way to protect people from smallpox?
    - ● Edward Jenner
    - Ⓑ Louis Pasteur
    - Ⓒ Gertrude Elion
    - Ⓓ Jonas Salk

Part 2: Skills Test

Directions: Use complete sentences to answer questions 1–4. Use a separate sheet of paper if you need more space.

1. What effect did improvements in transportation have on communities in the United States? **Cause and Effect**

   Possible answer: People and goods moved more quickly than they had in the past. People moved west, and more of the country developed because of changes in transportation.

2. What might have happened had the Transcontinental Railroad not been built? **Hypothesize**

   Possible answer: The country might not have grown as quickly. People would have had a harder time moving west.

3. What are at least three details to support this main idea? **The invention of the light bulb changed the way people lived. Main Idea and Details**

   Possible answer: Less danger from fire caused by candles burning at night, businesses and factories could stay open longer, people could see better at night

4. Which of the inventions from this chapter, such as the car, the telegraph, the light bulb, or the polio vaccine, do you think is the most important? Why? **Express Ideas**

   Possible answers should reflect an understanding of the impact of the chosen invention on humankind.

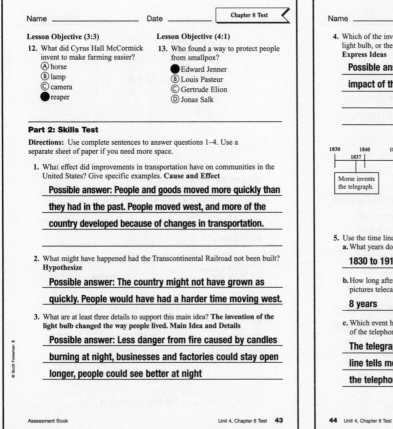

Communication Over Time

1830	1840	1850	1860	1870	1880	1890	1900	1910
	1837			1876		1896	1908	

- Morse invents the telegraph. (1837)
- Business people set up the Pony Express.
- Bell invents the first telephone. (1876)
- Marconi sends radio signals. (1896)
- Swinton telecasts words with black and white pictures. (1908)

5. Use the time line to answer the questions. **Use a Time Line**

   a. What years does the time line cover?

   1830 to 1910

   b. How long after Marconi sent radio signals were the first black and white pictures telecast?

   8 years

   c. Which event happened first: the invention of the telegraph or the invention of the telephone? How do you know?

   The telegraph was invented first. I know because the time line tells me that the telegraph was invented in 1837 and the telephone was invented in 1876.

Unit 4 Test

Part 1: Content Test

Directions: Fill in the circle next to the correct answer.

Lesson Objective (7–1:4)

1. How did the Iroquois obtain much of their food, such as corn?
   - ● The women were farmers.
   - Ⓑ The men were hunters.
   - Ⓒ The women were gatherers.
   - Ⓓ The men were farmers.

Lesson Objective (7–1:2, 3:2, 4:2)

2. Whom did the French, Spanish, and English all meet when they arrived in North America?
   - Ⓐ Ponce de León
   - Ⓑ Dutch settlers
   - ● Native Americans
   - Ⓓ Chief Powhatan

Lesson Objective (7–1:2)

3. Which of these explorers did NOT build a settlement in North America?
   - Ⓐ Christopher Columbus
   - Ⓑ Samuel de Champlain
   - Ⓒ Hernando de Soto
   - ● Jacques Cartier

Lesson Objective (7–2:1, 2)

4. Where did Ponce de León first land and explore?
   - Ⓐ in South America
   - ● north of present-day St. Augustine, Florida
   - Ⓒ near Quebec City, Quebec
   - Ⓓ east of Jamestown, Virginia

Lesson Objective (7–3:1, 2, 3)

5. What was the result of Jacques Cartier's exploration of Canada?
   - Ⓐ He built a settlement that is today a Canadian city.
   - Ⓑ He stayed at a castlelike hotel overlooking the St. Lawrence River.
   - ● He realized that there was no direct route to China.
   - Ⓓ He entertained people throughout Canada with his juggling act.

Lesson Objective (7–4:1, 2)

6. What settlement did Christopher Newport and the others who came with him build?
   - Ⓐ St. Augustine
   - ● Jamestown
   - Ⓒ Quebec City
   - Ⓓ Newfoundland

Lesson Objective (8–1:1)

7. Who told stories that made people want to move west in search of a better life?
   - Ⓐ Sacagawea and Powhatan
   - ● Lewis and Clark
   - Ⓒ Menéndez and Columbus
   - Ⓓ Cartier and Champlain

Lesson Objective (8–1:2)

8. What allowed people to travel on new roads and highways across America after 1903?
   - Ⓐ the airplane
   - Ⓑ the Transcontinental Railroad
   - Ⓒ the Oregon Trail
   - ● the automobile

Lesson Objective (8–2:2, 4)

9. Why was it important to Americans in the late 1700s that Benjamin Franklin set up post offices?
   - Ⓐ The Pony Express needed places for the riders and horses to rest.
   - ● In the 1800s people needed a better way to get a letter to families and friends.
   - Ⓒ Benjamin Franklin wanted to meet people all over the country.
   - Ⓓ Americans needed a place to pick up their mail after it arrived by train.

Lesson Objective (8–3:3)

10. How did the reaper help farmers of the 1800s?
    - ● Farming was made easier with a machine and a horse.
    - Ⓑ Farmers were able to take pictures of their fields.
    - Ⓒ Farmers could communicate quickly with others.
    - Ⓓ Farmers could walk through and harvest a field.

Lesson Objective (8–2:3)

11. How did Samuel Morse help Americans communicate faster?
    - Ⓐ He developed a way for people to be able to handwrite letters more quickly to family and friends.
    - Ⓑ His invention of email allowed people to use their computers to send messages around the world.
    - Ⓒ He set up the Pony Express, which delivered letters across the country more quickly than by wagon train.
    - ● He invented the telegraph, which could send messages across the country in just seconds.

Lesson Objective (8–3:1, 2)

12. How did Louis Daguerre change the way people remembered their favorite times?
    - Ⓐ He made drawings of a type of telephone.
    - Ⓑ He invented the light bulb and electric lamps.
    - Ⓒ He invented the reaper.
    - ● He invented a way to develop pictures.

Lesson Objective (8–4:2)

13. How does pasteurization help make milk safe to drink?
    - ● Milk is heated to the point that certain germs are killed.
    - Ⓑ Milk is injected with a very weak form of smallpox.
    - Ⓒ Milk is heated and mixed with the polio vaccine.
    - Ⓓ Milk is used to attack diseased cells.

Part 2: Skills Test

Directions: Use complete sentences to answer questions 1–3. Use a separate sheet of paper if you need more space.

1. How did the relationship between Juan Ponce de León and the Native Americans affect Spanish settlements in the area? **Express Ideas**

   De León and the Spanish attacked the Native Americans. The Native Americans attacked and killed De León, halting the settlement.

2. What are the major types of transportation that have been used in the United States? Write key events in the history of transportation in the order they happened. **Sequence**

   First walked and rode on horseback; then covered wagons; then trains; next Transcontinental Railroad, cars, and airplanes; today rockets, satellites, and space shuttles

3. What effect have vaccinations had on the lives of people today? **Cause and Effect**

   Lives have been saved. People are living longer because they do not catch certain diseases. People do not get sick as often.

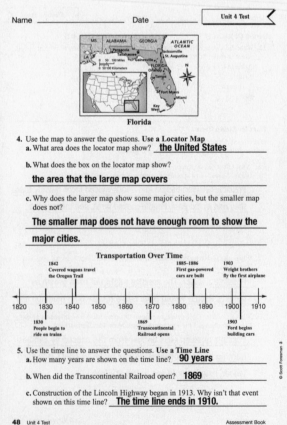

Florida

4. Use the map to answer the questions. **Use a Locator Map**
   a. What area does the locator map show? **the United States**

   b. What does the box on the locator map show?

   the area that the large map covers

   c. Why does the larger map show some major cities, but the smaller map does not?

   The smaller map does not have enough room to show the major cities.

Transportation Over Time

| 1842 Covered wagons travel the Oregon Trail | 1885–1886 First gas-powered cars are built | 1903 Wright brothers fly the first airplane |

1820 — 1830 — 1840 — 1850 — 1860 — 1870 — 1880 — 1890 — 1900 — 1910

| 1830 People begin to ride on trains | 1869 Transcontinental Railroad opens | 1903 Ford begins building cars |

5. Use the time line to answer the questions. **Use a Time Line**
   a. How many years are shown on the time line? **90 years**

   b. When did the Transcontinental Railroad open? **1869**

   c. Construction of the Lincoln Highway began in 1913. Why isn't that event shown on this time line? **The time line ends in 1910.**

© Scott Foresman 3

84 Answer Key | Assessment Book

Chapter 9 Test

Part 1: Content Test

Directions: Fill in the circle next to the correct answer.

Lesson Objective (1:1)

1. Which is a way to earn money?
   - ● walk your neighbor's dog
   - Ⓑ buy a new softball bat
   - Ⓒ save money in a bank
   - Ⓓ buy two CDs for $20

Lesson Objective (1:1)

2. Which is NOT a way to spend money?
   - Ⓐ buy your own lunch in your school cafeteria
   - Ⓑ give your brother $10 for his birthday
   - ● run errands for your older neighbors
   - Ⓓ donate $5 a week to your church offering

Lesson Objective (1:2)

3. Which three columns are important to have on a budget?
   - Ⓐ Wants, Needs, and Supplies
   - ● Income, Spending, and Saving
   - Ⓒ Softballs, Bats, and Gloves
   - Ⓓ Week 1, Week 2, and Week 3

Lesson Objective (1:3)

4. What is a *need*?
   - Ⓐ A need is something you would like but can live without.
   - Ⓑ A need is a plan that shows income, spending, and saving.
   - Ⓒ A need is the amount of money a person uses each day.
   - ● A need is something that a person must have to live.

Lesson Objective (1:3)

5. Which of the following is an example of a *want*?
   - ● a softball bat
   - Ⓑ fresh water
   - Ⓒ food to eat
   - Ⓓ a place to live

Lesson Objective (2:1)

6. Which is an example of an economic choice?
   - ● Robin chooses to buy a softball bat instead of two CDs.
   - Ⓑ Robin chooses to sit by her sister at lunch instead of by her friends.
   - Ⓒ Robin chooses to play softball instead of basketball.
   - Ⓓ Robin chooses to eat chicken nuggets instead of a hamburger at lunch.

Lesson Objective (2:2)

7. Why did Robin make a chart about softball bats?
   - Ⓐ to give to the owner of the sporting goods store
   - ● to help her decide which one she should buy
   - Ⓒ to show her father how to make a chart
   - Ⓓ to prepare for her test on softball bats

Lesson Objective (2:3)

8. What was Robin's opportunity cost when she bought the softball bat?
   - Ⓐ a softball
   - Ⓑ ten bats
   - ● two CDs
   - Ⓓ a T-ball bat

Lesson Objective (2:3)

9. Suppose that your mother buys a pair of shoes instead of a jacket. What is her opportunity cost?
   - Ⓐ the pair of shoes
   - Ⓑ a pair of socks
   - ● the jacket
   - Ⓓ two CDs

Lesson Objective (3:3)

10. Which is a good that a sporting goods store might sell?
    - ● a softball bat
    - Ⓑ baseball lessons
    - Ⓒ umpire for games
    - Ⓓ people to sew uniforms

Lesson Objective (3:1)

11. What usually happens when the supply of a product goes up?
    - Ⓐ The price of that product also goes up.
    - Ⓑ The demand for that product also goes up.
    - Ⓒ The producers of that product make more of it.
    - ● The price of that product goes down.

Lesson Objective (3:1)

12. What might a store owner do if few people are buying a certain product?
    - Ⓐ The store owner might open a new store for the product.
    - Ⓑ The store owner might raise the price of the product.
    - ● The store owner might lower the price of the product.
    - Ⓓ The store owner might order more of the product.

Lesson Objective (3:2)

13. What is *profit*?
    - ● the income a business has left after all its costs are paid
    - Ⓑ the money that a business spends over the course of a year
    - Ⓒ the amount of a product that people want and can pay for
    - Ⓓ the amount of money a business brings in

Lesson Objective (3:2)

14. What must a business do in order to make a profit?
    - Ⓐ It has to spend more money than it is able to save.
    - Ⓑ It has to supply more products than people demand.
    - ● It has to sell a product for more than the cost to make it.
    - Ⓓ It has to provide a service to the community.

Lesson Objective (3:2, 3)

15. What is one thing that a store owner can do to increase profit?
    - Ⓐ sell goods at a lower price
    - Ⓑ provide services for free
    - Ⓒ increase the supply of goods
    - ● sell goods at a higher price

Part 2: Skills Test

Directions: Use complete sentences to answer questions 1–5. Use a separate sheet of paper if you need more space.

1. Suppose you want to buy a new keyboard, but you need to save for the purchase. Describe, in the order in which they happen, the events involved in creating and using a budget to save for the keyboard. **Sequence**

   First, I would draw a chart with three columns: Income, Spending, and Saving. Next, I would fill in what I earned in the first week. I would think about what I spend. I would decide how much to save. I would estimate how many weeks I need to save.

2. Think about your last trip to the grocery store or mall. What did you or your family buy? Which items were needs and which items were wants? **Categorize**

   Students' classifications should reflect an understanding of needs and wants.

3. Suppose that your school principal has $5,000 to spend. She could buy new computers, new books for the library, or new playground equipment. Which do you think she should buy? Why? **Apply Information**

   Possible answer: The books, because everyone can enjoy more books

4. Suppose that you earned $25 for walking a neighbor's dog last month. Will you spend the money or save it? If you spend some of it, what will you buy? What steps will you take in deciding what to do with your money? Write the steps in the order in which they will happen. **Sequence**

   Possible answer: First, I have to decide if I must spend any money on my needs. Then I have to decide what I want to buy. I would then make a budget to help me plan to use my money. I will research what I want. I will find the best price. I will spend my money.

5. Suppose a store in your community sells only soccer equipment. What might happen to the store if community interest in soccer decreases? Why? What can the store owner do to solve this problem? **Cause and Effect**

   The store will not make as much money because it will not sell as many soccer items. The store owner might have a sale or start a new league. The owner might decide to carry other products to make up for the equipment that is not selling well.

Chapter 10 Test

Part 1: Content Test

Directions: Fill in the circle next to the correct answer.

Lesson Objective (1:1)

1. Which natural resource is used to make a softball bat?
   - Ⓐ fish
   - ● trees
   - Ⓒ coal
   - Ⓓ oil

Lesson Objective (1:1)

2. Which is NOT a capital resource?
   - Ⓐ a building where bats are made
   - Ⓑ a computer that runs a machine
   - ● a worker who shapes bats by hand
   - Ⓓ a machine that cuts softball bats

Lesson Objective (1:2)

3. How can computerized machines help a business make greater profits?
   - Ⓐ The machines are expensive and cost the company a lot of money.
   - Ⓑ The company can track its spending on the computer.
   - ● Making products more quickly can cost the company less money.
   - Ⓓ Machines can make people buy more of the company's product.

Lesson Objective (1:3)

4. What must happen before a worker can sand a piece of wood to make a softball bat?
   - Ⓐ A worker must dip the bat into colored paint.
   - Ⓑ Someone must go to the store and buy the softball bat.
   - Ⓒ A computerized machine must sand the piece of wood.
   - ● A tree must be cut down and split into lumber.

Lesson Objective (2:1)

5. What does it mean to say a resource is "scarce"?
   - Ⓐ There is too much of it.
   - ● There is not enough of it.
   - Ⓒ There is a lot of it.
   - Ⓓ There is none of it.

Lesson Objective (2:1)

6. Which of these is NOT a resource that is scarce?
   - Ⓐ wood
   - Ⓑ gasoline
   - Ⓒ coal
   - ● sunshine

Lesson Objective (2:2)

7. What might happen if a community chooses to use wood to build a new playground?
   - ● There might not be enough wood for something else.
   - Ⓑ Many new trees might grow on the playground.
   - Ⓒ There might not be enough gasoline to power people's cars.
   - Ⓓ The lumber company might not make enough profit.

Lesson Objective (2:3)

8. For which resource does Phoenix, Arizona, have to depend on Portland, Oregon?
   - Ⓐ water
   - ● wood
   - Ⓒ coal
   - Ⓓ oil

Lesson Objective (2:4)

9. What happens before lumber is delivered to a community?
   - Ⓐ A community builds a fence.
   - Ⓑ Furniture is made from the lumber.
   - Ⓒ A driver unloads the lumber.
   - ● Trees are cut down and milled.

Lesson Objective (2:4)

10. Who provides a service that allows lumber to get to cities around the country?
    - ● truck driver
    - Ⓑ bat maker
    - Ⓒ umpire
    - Ⓓ letter carrier

Lesson Objective (3:2)

11. Which is NOT a reason why people trade with each other?
    - Ⓐ to get goods they cannot make
    - Ⓑ to make money from the trade
    - Ⓒ to benefit from the trade
    - ● to travel and meet new people

Lesson Objective (3:1)

12. What is *communication*?
    - ● sharing of information or news
    - Ⓑ buying of goods and services
    - Ⓒ trading between two countries
    - Ⓓ sending of goods to a country

Lesson Objective (3:1, 3)

13. Which of the following is one way goods were transported during ancient times and today?
    - Ⓐ by train
    - Ⓑ by truck
    - ● by ship
    - Ⓓ by airplane

Lesson Objective (3:3)

14. Which was a specialty of the people of ancient Rome?
    - ● building ships
    - Ⓑ farming
    - Ⓒ making softball bats
    - Ⓓ selling

Part 2: Skills Test

Directions: Use complete sentences to answer questions 1–4. Use a separate sheet of paper if you need more space.

1. What natural resources do you use at school? What human resources and capital resources do you use? **Categorize**

   Possible answers: Natural resources—trees (furniture, paper, pencils); oil, electricity, or gas (heating and cooling); water; Human resources—teachers, principal, coaches, librarian; Capital resources—buildings, playground equipment, computers, desks, buses

2. Suppose you are the leader of Robin's community. What steps would you have to take in deciding what to do with your community's land? Write those steps in the order in which they would occur. **Sequence**

   Possible answer: I would ask people for ideas on how they would like to use the land. Next, I would see how much each of their ideas would cost. Then I would share that information with the community. I would have the citizens of the community vote on which idea they like the best. Finally, I would ask a group of people to carry out the idea.

3. What are three examples to support the following main idea? **In the United States, people and companies are part of a free market.** Main Idea and Details

   Possible answer: Farmers decide which crops to plant; people decide to buy or sell their own homes; store owners decide which products to sell.

4. Often when countries disagree, they refuse to trade with each other. What effect might such disagreements have on the people who live in those countries? **Cause and Effect**

   If the country stops importing important products, such as oil or food, life might be very different without those products. The prices of these goods might also rise because the supply would decrease.

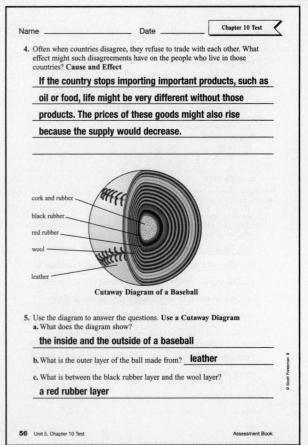

cork and rubber
black rubber
red rubber
wool
leather

Cutaway Diagram of a Baseball

5. Use the diagram to answer the questions. **Use a Cutaway Diagram**
   a. What does the diagram show?

   the inside and the outside of a baseball

   b. What is the outer layer of the ball made from? **leather**

   c. What is between the black rubber layer and the wool layer?

   a red rubber layer

© Scott Foresman 3

Unit 5 Test

Part 1: Content Test

Directions: Fill in the circle next to the correct answer.

Lesson Objective (9–1:2)

1. Which is NOT something that would be found on a budget?
   - Ⓐ the amount of money you saved last week
   - Ⓑ the amount of money you earned babysitting
   - Ⓒ the amount of money you spent on a gift
   - ● the amount of money you want to spend on a new bat

Lesson Objective (9–1:3)

2. How does a want differ from a need?
   - ● A want is something you would like to have but can live without.
   - Ⓑ A want is something made of wood, such as a softball bat.
   - Ⓒ A want is something that you must have in order to live.
   - Ⓓ A want is something made from a nonrenewable resource.

Lesson Objective (9–2:1)

3. Which is NOT an example of an economic choice?
   - Ⓐ Your school buys computers instead of science equipment.
   - Ⓑ Your mother buys a loaf of bread instead of rolls.
   - ● Your sister wears her red boots instead of her tennis shoes.
   - Ⓓ Your community builds a playground instead of a swimming pool.

Lesson Objective (9–2:3)

4. What is an opportunity cost?
   - Ⓐ something you would like to have but can live without
   - ● what you give up when you choose one thing instead of another
   - Ⓒ a plan to help you track your earning and spending
   - Ⓓ when you buy one thing instead of another

Lesson Objective (9–3:1)

5. What might happen if the demand for a product were to go up?
   - Ⓐ The production of that product might stop.
   - Ⓑ The supply of that product might stay the same.
   - Ⓒ The price of that product might go down.
   - ● The price of that product might go up.

Lesson Objective (10–1:1)

6. Which is NOT an example of a human resource?
   - ● a computer that cuts bats
   - Ⓑ a woman who sands bats
   - Ⓒ a man who umpires a game
   - Ⓓ an employee of a sporting goods store

Lesson Objective (9–3:2, 3; 10–1:2)

7. What might happen if a softball bat maker has to increase pay for its workers?
   - Ⓐ The bat maker probably will have a sale on softball bats.
   - ● Unless it also charges its customers more, it will lose some of its profits.
   - Ⓒ The owner might have to give the bats to customers for free.
   - Ⓓ Because of the price of making bats, it will make only balls.

Lesson Objective (10–2:1, 2, 3)

8. Why is Portland, Oregon, important to Phoenix, Arizona?
   - Ⓐ Because there are so many trees in Arizona, communities there send their logs to mills in Portland.
   - Ⓑ Because trees are scarce, communities in Arizona build products out of metal and sell them in Portland.
   - ● Because trees are scarce, communities in Arizona must get their lumber from places such as Portland.
   - Ⓓ Because there are so many trees in Arizona, communities there share their lumber with Portland.

Lesson Objective (10–3:1)

9. How has communication helped increase trade?
   - ● If a grocery store needs goods quickly, it can email its suppliers.
   - Ⓑ People can now move goods quickly around the world.
   - Ⓒ Today people often trade goods and services for money.
   - Ⓓ People now can buy and sell services.

Lesson Objective (10–3:2)

10. Which is NOT a reason why people trade with each other?
   - ● to get something they can already make for themselves
   - Ⓑ to make money from selling their goods and services
   - Ⓒ to get something they cannot make or grow for themselves
   - Ⓓ to find goods they can use in making other goods

Lesson Objective (10–3:4)

11. How is the market in some other countries different from the market in the United States?
   - Ⓐ In other countries people choose what to produce.
   - Ⓑ In other countries people choose what to buy.
   - ● In some countries the government decides what is bought and sold.
   - Ⓓ In other countries people and companies are a part of a free market.

Part 2: Skills Test

Directions: Use complete sentences to answer questions 1–4. Use a separate sheet of paper if you need more space.

1. Think of a large purchase you would like to make. What steps should you take before buying that item? Write, in the order in which they happen, the steps to creating a budget and making an economic choice. **Sequence**

   Possible answer: I would find out how much money I needed, make a budget, find ways to earn money, and work to earn the money I needed.

2. Suppose a business were to pay its workers less money than it had in the past. How might it affect other businesses in the community? **Cause and Effect**

   The workers would have less money to spend for food, clothing, and housing, so businesses that supply those things might earn less money.

3. Why is it important to use natural resources wisely? Human and capital resources? How might human and capital resources be used wisely? **Make Inferences**

   Natural resources should be used wisely so we do not run out of them. A business could not survive without human resources to make goods and provide services. Capital resources usually are expensive. If used unwisely, they might break and be costly to replace.

4. Would you like to live in a country that does not have a free market? Why or why not? **Make Decisions**

   Possible answer: No, because I want the freedom to choose what I produce and what I buy

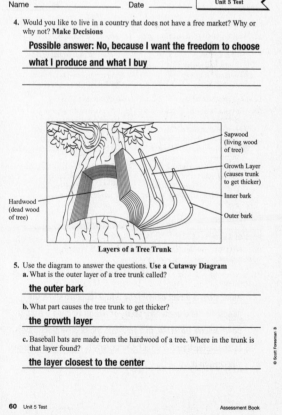

Layers of a Tree Trunk

5. Use the diagram to answer the questions. **Use a Cutaway Diagram**
   a. What is the outer layer of a tree trunk called?

   the outer bark

   b. What part causes the tree trunk to get thicker?

   the growth layer

   c. Baseball bats are made from the hardwood of a tree. Where in the trunk is that layer found?

   the layer closest to the center

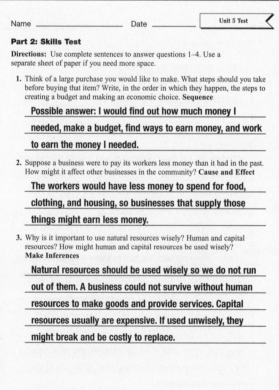

Chapter 11 Test

Part 1: Content Test

Directions: Fill in the circle next to the correct answer.

Lesson Objective (1:1)

1. Which is NOT a reason why the people of ancient Greece formed a community?
   - Ⓐ to have a safe place to work
   - Ⓑ to have a safe place to live
   - Ⓒ to live under a set of fair laws
   - ● to form a republic

Lesson Objective (1:2)

2. What is one way government buildings in Washington, D.C., compare with those in ancient Greece?
   - Ⓐ Both were built on the water.
   - Ⓑ Both look like small houses.
   - ● Both have a similar style of architecture.
   - Ⓓ Both lack a roof.

Lesson Objective (1:3)

3. How does the government of ancient Greece differ from the U.S. government?
   - Ⓐ Both countries are run by kings.
   - ● Greece had a direct democracy; the United States has a republic.
   - Ⓒ Greece had a republic; the United States has a direct democracy.
   - Ⓓ Greece had no form of government, but the United States does.

Lesson Objective (1:4)

4. Where can many of the ideas from the Magna Carta be found today?
   - ● in the U.S. Constitution
   - Ⓑ in the Mayflower Compact
   - Ⓒ in the home of King John
   - Ⓓ in Greek laws

Lesson Objective (1:4)

5. What did the Mayflower Compact say?
   - Ⓐ Only the King of England could make laws.
   - ● The colonists themselves would make laws.
   - Ⓒ The Magna Carta would no longer be in effect.
   - Ⓓ The people of Athens could live in a republic.

Lesson Objective (2:1)

6. What did the Declaration of Independence say?
   - Ⓐ The government of England was always right and fair.
   - Ⓑ The colonists would all go back to live in England.
   - Ⓒ The Mayflower Compact could not be used in the colonies.
   - ● The colonies were free and no longer part of England.

Lesson Objective (2:2)

7. Which is NOT true about the U.S. Constitution?
   - Ⓐ It was a plan for our government.
   - Ⓑ James Madison helped write it.
   - ● King John agreed with its ideas.
   - Ⓓ It gives the power to the people.

Lesson Objective (2:4)

8. Who was chosen to make plans for Washington, D.C.?
   - Ⓐ George Washington
   - ● Pierre Charles L'Enfant
   - Ⓒ Thomas Jefferson
   - Ⓓ Thurgood Marshall

Lesson Objective (2:3)

9. What is included in the Bill of Rights?
   - ● protection of the people's rights
   - Ⓑ fifteen amendments to the Constitution
   - Ⓒ the declaration of independence from England
   - Ⓓ the point of view of the king of England

Lesson Objective (2:5)

10. How did Rosa Parks help change her community?
    - ● She believed that all people's rights should be protected and, in time, they were.
    - Ⓑ She liked to ride the bus to work, and she encouraged others to ride it too.
    - Ⓒ She sewed new clothes for every person who lived in her community.
    - Ⓓ She was the first member of her community to serve on the U.S. Supreme Court.

Lesson Objective (2:6)

11. How do you know that Rosa Parks and Thurgood Marshall were good citizens?
    - Ⓐ They both refused to give up a seat on the bus.
    - Ⓑ They both lived and worked in Washington, D.C.
    - Ⓒ They both rode the bus to work each day.
    - ● They both showed a belief in equality and justice.

Lesson Objective (3:1, 2)

12. Which is NOT a responsibility of a good citizen?
    - Ⓐ obeying laws
    - Ⓑ voting in elections
    - ● running for office
    - Ⓓ paying taxes

Lesson Objective (3:2, 3)

13. What should a good citizen do after an election?
    - Ⓐ A good citizen should be angry if his or her favorite candidate lost.
    - ● A good citizen should accept the results of the election.
    - Ⓒ A good citizen should count all the votes that were cast.
    - Ⓓ A good citizen should work to defeat the new leader in the next election.

Lesson Objective (3:5)

14. How can you help decide how your student government is run?
    - Ⓐ vote in city elections
    - Ⓑ vote in county elections
    - Ⓒ complain to other students
    - ● vote in school elections

Lesson Objective (3:4)

15. What is something you can do to improve your community?
    - ● You can volunteer to help people who are hungry.
    - Ⓑ You can throw trash and food in the streets.
    - Ⓒ You can obey only those laws that you think are fair.
    - Ⓓ You cannot personally do anything to improve a community.

Part 2: Skills Test

Directions: Use complete sentences to answer questions 1–5. Use a separate sheet of paper if you need more space.

1. How is a direct democracy like a republic? How is it different? **Compare and Contrast**

   Alike: both a direct democracy and a republic allow the people of the community, state, or nation to have a part in government. Different: in a republic the people elect others to speak for them. A direct democracy is run by the citizens who live in it.

2. What are five documents that are important to our country's history? List them in the order in which they were written. **Sequence**

   The five documents are the Magna Carta, the Mayflower Compact, the Declaration of Independence, the U.S. Constitution, and the Bill of Rights.

3. What was Thomas Jefferson's point of view about England? How do you know? **Summarize**

   Jefferson did not think England should govern the colonies. We know this because he helped write the Declaration of Independence, the document that said the colonies were free and no longer part of England.

4. Suppose that a summary you are writing has the following main idea: **Rosa Parks and Thurgood Marshall were good citizens.** What details would you include in your summary? **Main Idea and Details**

   Possible answers: Both worked to better their communities; both worked to make sure people were treated fairly; both believed in equality and justice.

5. What are three things that you can do to make your community a better place in which to live? **Apply Information**

   Accept all reasonable answers. Possible answers: Respect the rights and property of others; obey laws; pay taxes; vote in school elections.

© Scott Foresman 3

Chapter 12 Test
Part 1: Content Test
Directions: Fill in the circle next to the correct answer.

Lesson Objective (1:1)

1. Which is NOT one of the services people expect from their government?
   - Ⓐ education
   - Ⓑ transportation
   - ● communication
   - Ⓓ recreation

Lesson Objective (1:1)

2. How can a local government meet people's need for safety?
   - Ⓐ by building a nature center
   - ● by operating a police department
   - Ⓒ by planting trees in the community
   - Ⓓ by forming a city or town council

Lesson Objective (1:2)

3. Which of the following is an educational service provided by many local governments?
   - Ⓐ police departments
   - Ⓑ sports leagues
   - ● libraries
   - Ⓓ senior centers

Lesson Objective (1:4)

4. Which is NOT a form of recreation provided by local governments?
   - Ⓐ parks
   - Ⓑ swimming pools
   - ● schools
   - Ⓓ senior centers

Lesson Objective (1:3)

5. How can a local government make transportation easier for its citizens?
   - Ⓐ by building a swimming pool
   - Ⓑ by adding books to the library
   - ● by building and fixing roads
   - Ⓓ by picking up citizens' trash

Lesson Objective (1:5)

6. What is one way local governments get money to pay for the services they provide?
   - ● They charge fees for some services.
   - Ⓑ They invest in the stock market.
   - Ⓒ They ask for donations.
   - Ⓓ They do not pay for the services they provide.

Lesson Objective (2:2)

7. How are the members of a town or city council chosen?
   - ● Adults in the community vote.
   - Ⓑ The mayor chooses them.
   - Ⓒ The school board chooses them.
   - Ⓓ People take a test to become members.

Lesson Objective (2:2)

8. Which of the following can veto a bill?
   - Ⓐ mayor
   - Ⓑ chief
   - Ⓒ police officer
   - ● governor

Lesson Objective (2:1)

9. Which is NOT usually a job of the mayor and the city council?
   - Ⓐ deciding what they want the local government to do
   - Ⓑ picking people to provide services
   - Ⓒ choosing the police chief and the fire chief
   - ● running the police department and the fire department

Lesson Objective (2:2)

10. How are community leaders able to make and carry out laws?
    - Ⓐ Candidates read books about carrying out laws.
    - Ⓑ The mayor demands that citizens obey laws.
    - Ⓒ The leaders take a class about making laws.
    - ● People give their consent to the leaders.

Lesson Objective (2:3)

11. What happens if an elected leader does not do a good job?
    - ● The people may not vote for that person in the next election.
    - Ⓑ The person must give his or her position to someone else.
    - Ⓒ The person must serve on the town council for two more years.
    - Ⓓ The people may elect that person mayor at the next election.

Lesson Objective (3:1, 2, 4)

12. After a governor vetoes a bill, what might happen?
    - Ⓐ the bill becomes law
    - ● the Legislative branch votes on the bill again
    - Ⓒ the bill goes to another branch of government
    - Ⓓ the governor rewrites the bill

Lesson Objective (3:2, 4)

13. What is one way a person can improve his or her community?
    - Ⓐ by disobeying the laws of the community
    - Ⓑ by never voting in community elections
    - ● by picking up trash in the community
    - Ⓓ by driving fast on busy streets in the community

Lesson Objective (3:1, 3, 5)

14. What two groups of lawmakers make up most state Legislatures?
    - ● the House of Representatives and the Senate
    - Ⓑ the Judicial branch and the Executive branch
    - Ⓒ the Senate and the governor
    - Ⓓ Judges and juries

Part 2: Skills Test
Directions: Use complete sentences to answer questions 1–4. Use a separate sheet of paper if you need more space.

1. Suppose that you are writing a summary about the services that local governments provide. What is your summary's main idea? What is one detail from your summary? **Summarize**

   Possible answers: Local governments provide services to make the community a better place; local governments provide fire and police departments.

2. When you are older, you probably will have to pay taxes to your local government. How do you feel about taxes? Are they important? Should every citizen have to pay them? Why or why not? **Express Ideas**

   Possible answers: I think some taxes are necessary to pay for community services; people who use these services should pay taxes; it is not fair to make people pay for services they do not use.

3. Name at least three offices in local government. Tell whether each position is elected or chosen. **Categorize**

   Elected officials include council members, mayor (sometimes), school board members, and park district board members. Chosen officials include mayor (sometimes), police chief, fire chief, and school superintendent.

---

4. Would you like to work for your local government when you are older? Why or why not? What position would you like to hold? **Apply Information**

   Accept all reasonable answers. Possible answers: Yes; because I want to help my community run smoothly; police chief

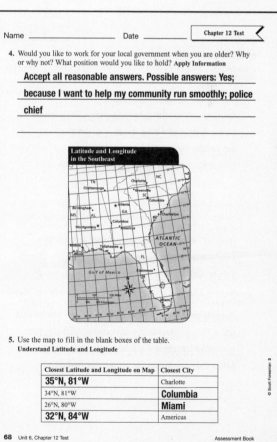

Latitude and Longitude in the Southeast

5. Use the map to fill in the blank boxes of the table.
   Understand Latitude and Longitude

Closest Latitude and Longitude on Map	Closest City
35°N, 81°W	Charlotte
34°N, 81°W	**Columbia**
26°N, 80°W	**Miami**
32°N, 84°W	Americus

Unit 6 Test

Part 1: Content Test

Directions: Fill in the circle next to the correct answer.

Lesson Objective (11–1:2)

1. Where did architects in Washington, D.C., get many of their ideas for designing government buildings?
   Ⓐ from the Magna Carta
   Ⓑ from the Mayflower Compact
   Ⓒ from stories about ancient Greece
   ● from buildings in ancient Greece

Lesson Objective (11–1:1, 3)

2. How did the citizens of ancient Athens know that their community would have fair laws?
   ● The citizens created their own laws.
   Ⓑ The citizens elected fair officials to create laws.
   Ⓒ The citizens knew that their king would make fair laws.
   Ⓓ The citizens lived under the rules of the Magna Carta.

Lesson Objective (11–1:4)

3. Which two documents influenced the founders of our country?
   Ⓐ the Mayflower Compact and the *Mayflower*
   Ⓑ the Mayflower Compact and ancient Greece
   Ⓒ the Magna Carta and a letter from King John
   ● the Magna Carta and the Mayflower Compact

Lesson Objective (11–2:1, 2, 3)

4. Which is NOT a document important to the United States?
   Ⓐ Bill of Rights
   Ⓑ U.S. Constitution
   ● U.S. Capitol
   Ⓓ Declaration of Independence

Lesson Objective (11–2:4)

5. What did Pierre Charles L'Enfant do?
   ● He made the plans for Washington, D.C.
   Ⓑ He built the U.S. Capitol building by hand.
   Ⓒ He was the first President of our country.
   Ⓓ He helped Jefferson with the Bill of Rights.

Lesson Objective (11–2:5, 6)

6. How was Rosa Parks different from Thurgood Marshall?
   Ⓐ Rosa Parks believed in equality and justice.
   Ⓑ Rosa Parks was a good citizen of her community.
   Ⓒ Rosa Parks helped change our country.
   ● Rosa Parks refused to give up her seat on a bus.

Lesson Objective (11–3:2)

7. How should every good citizen help his or her elected leaders?
   ● by obeying the laws that leaders pass
   Ⓑ by working on a leader's staff
   Ⓒ by giving all of his or her money to the leaders
   Ⓓ by running for office

Lesson Objective (11–3:2, 3)

8. Which is a responsibility of a good citizen?
   Ⓐ deciding what property others may keep
   Ⓑ disobeying laws
   ● voting in elections
   Ⓓ running for office

Lesson Objective (12–1:1)

9. Which is NOT a kind of service that local governments often provide to citizens?
   Ⓐ education
   Ⓑ transportation
   ● communication
   Ⓓ recreation

Lesson Objective (12–1:5)

10. How might your family help your local government pay for the services it provides?
    Ⓐ by buying a traffic signal
    ● by paying for trash pickup
    Ⓒ by connecting to the Internet
    Ⓓ by refusing to pay taxes

Lesson Objective (11–3:4)

11. How can a student help improve his or her school?
    Ⓐ try to use as many school supplies as possible
    Ⓑ refuse to obey his or her teacher and principal
    ● vote for leaders to run the student government
    Ⓓ attend his or her classes regularly

Lesson Objective (12–2:1, 2)

12. How are city council members usually chosen?
    Ⓐ Candidates take a social studies test.
    Ⓑ The police chief chooses council members.
    ● Adults in a community vote for local leaders.
    Ⓓ Local teachers decide who is the smartest.

Lesson Objective (12–2:3)

13. How do voters give their consent to their leaders?
    Ⓐ by running behind their leaders
    Ⓑ by cheering for their leaders
    Ⓒ by writing their leaders a letter
    ● by electing their leaders to office

Part 2: Skills Test

Directions: Use complete sentences to answer questions 1–4. Use a separate sheet of paper if you need more space.

1. Why do you think other countries have used our Constitution as a guide when setting up their governments? **Make Inferences**

   Possible answer: Our Constitution gives the power to the people instead of a king. It makes sure that every citizen has certain rights. Also, our country has worked well and prospered under our Constitution for over 200 years.

2. Suppose that you are writing a summary about being a good citizen. What is your main idea? What is one detail from your summary? **Summarize**

   Possible answers: Good citizens work to make their community a better place in which to live; good citizens vote for leaders who will help the community run smoothly.

3. What services does your local government provide for its citizens? Tell whether each is an education, recreation, transportation, or safety service. **Categorize**

   Possible answers: My local government provides schools and a library (education), a park and a swimming pool (recreation), roads and sidewalks (transportation), and a police department and fire department (safety).

---

4. Suppose that while playing at a city park, you notice that the playground is unsafe. How can you help solve this problem? **Solve Problems**

   Possible answers: Write a letter to the city council to have it fix the problem; fix the problem myself; get others to help me fix the problem

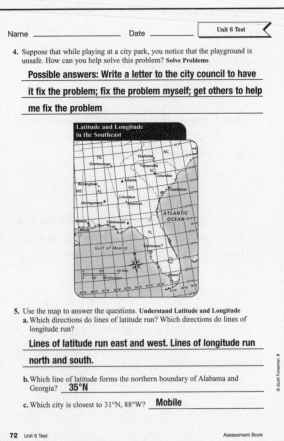

Latitude and Longitude in the Southeast

5. Use the map to answer the questions. **Understand Latitude and Longitude**
   a. Which directions do lines of latitude run? Which directions do lines of longitude run?

   Lines of latitude run east and west. Lines of longitude run north and south.

   b. Which line of latitude forms the northern boundary of Alabama and Georgia? **35°N**

   c. Which city is closest to 31°N, 88°W? **Mobile**

© Scott Foresman 3

NOTES

NOTES

NOTES

NOTES

NOTES

NOTES

NOTES

NOTES

NOTES

NOTES

NOTES

NOTES

NOTES

NOTES